Babe Ruth's Own Book of Baseball

© *Acme*

GEORGE HERMAN RUTH

BABE RUTH'S
Own Book of Baseball

By

GEORGE HERMAN RUTH

With 31 Illustrations

Introduction to the Bison Book Edition
by Jerome Holtzman

University of Nebraska Press
Lincoln and London

Introduction copyright © 1992 by the University of Nebraska Press
Manufactured in the United States of America

First Bison Book printing: 1992
Most recent printing indicated by the last digit below:
10   9   8   7   6   5   4   3   2

Library of Congress Cataloging-in-Publication Data
Ruth, Babe, 1895–1948.
Babe Ruth's own book of baseball / by George Herman Ruth;
introduction to the Bison Book edition by Jerome Holtzman.
p.   cm.
Reprint. Originally published: New York: G.P. Putnam's Sons,
1928.
"Bison."
ISBN 0-8032-3905-X.—ISBN 0-8032-8939-1 (pbk.)
1. Baseball. 2. Ruth, Babe, 1895–1948. I. Title. II. Title: Book of
baseball.
GV867.R8   1992
796.357—dc20   91-38383
CIP

Reprinted from the original 1928 edition published by
G. P. Putnam's Sons, New York

Introduction

By Jerome Holtzman

Last summer, in June 1991, two Babe Ruth movies were filmed, simultaneously, one for the theaters, the other for television. When I discovered one was being shot at Chicago's Wrigley Field I called for the production schedule and asked when the Babe would point.

As the baseball columnist for the *Chicago Tribune*, it occurred to me that, fifty-nine years later, I would have the opportunity to witness the Babe call his shot. I am enough of a baseball bibliophile to know he didn't point. It's the biggest hoax in the history of American sports.

Anyhow, I watched the actor John Goodman, outfitted in Babe's No. 3, waddle to the plate and lift a defiant finger toward the center field bleachers. Unlike the Babe, Goodman didn't hit the ball; the filmmakers can handle that. When the movie comes out, the next scene will show a ball in flight and so on, a joyous and grinning Babe circling the bases in triumph.

It never happened, I said in my column the next morning. Then came the surprise. I am in my fifth decade as a baseball writer and probably receive an ordinary amount of mail, usually a dozen letters a week. The reaction to the Babe column was enormous.

Only once before have I had a near-similar response. In 1969 when the Cubs blew the pennant I called the players crybabies. They were constantly whining against Leo Durocher, their ogre manager who had been bruising their egos. By coincidence, when he was a young player with the Yankees, Durocher allegedly stole the Babe's watch from his clubhouse locker.

Whether true or false, Stanley Frank, a well-known New York sportswriter of the time, ran with it: "The Name of the Game," a short story that appeared in the old *Saturday Evening Post*. Protecting himself from libel, Frank clothed the piece in fiction. Nonetheless, Durocher could read. Years later, when they met again, in a hotel hallway, Durocher almost threw a punch.

But that's another story. What we must remember, if we had forgotten as I have, is that the Babe lives. He died in 1948, almost a half century ago. Roger Maris broke his one-season home run record in 1961 and thirteen years later Hank Aaron passed him in the most home runs, lifetime—events that should have lost the Babe in the fog of time. Instead, he is as large as ever. What other sports figure would be the subject, in the same summer, of dueling films?

There have been two generations of baseball fans since the Babe's time. Only senior citizens, age seventy and beyond, could have seen him in his prime. Often, at that age, memories diminish. Not so when it comes to the Babe. Of the hundreds of letter-writers, easily more than half reported they were at the game and saw the Babe point. The home run was to right center. But several of the correspondents insisted that the ball dropped near where they sat—in left field.

Ruth was a hero of gargantuan proportions, so much so that I am reminded of my interview with Paul Gallico in the early '70s for *No Cheering in the Press Box*, an assemblage of reminiscences of retired sportswriters. Gallico had surfaced as a sportswriter but switched to fiction before he was forty. In explaining how the story of Babe's pointing was perpetuated, Gallico said: "People are like children. What a child likes best is to hear the same fairy tale told over and over again. And when Mommy leaves out something, the kid says, 'Oh, but Mommy, you forgot where the dwarf said so-and-so.' Grown-ups are like that, too."

The Hollywood crew was ferocious in defending the myth. A spokesman, in a burst of honesty later denied, told me that a 16-millimiter home film of the event recently had surfaced but wasn't publicized until 1988. "It's kind of grainy," he admitted. "Nor is it conclusive. You can't really tell."

As time went on, the Babe fueled the legend. The Hall of Fame in Cooperstown has a tape of the Babe saying:

> "Charlie Root was pitching and the pitched ball was a called strike. Well, I thought it was outside and didn't like it very much and the boys over there [in the Cub dugout] were giving me an 'Ooija! Ooija!' Well, the second pitch was another called strike and I didn't like that one very much, either. By that time they [the Cub players] were going crazy. So I stepped out of the box and looked out toward center field and I pointed and I said 'I'm gonna hit the next pitched ball right past the flagpole.' And that's what I did."

The tape was made several years before the Babe died. He offered a considerably different version in the spring of 1933, six months after the supposed call shot. In an interview with Hal Totten, a Chicago broadcaster, Ruth said:

> "Hell no, I didn't point. Only a damned fool would do a thing like that. You know there was a lot of pretty rough ribbing going on on both benches. When I swung and missed that first one, those Cubs really gave me a blast. So I grinned at 'em and held out one finger and told 'em it'd take only one to hit it.
>
> "Then there was that second strike and they let me have it again. So I held up that finger again and I said I still had one left.

INTRODUCTION

Naw, keed, you know damn well I wasn't pointin' anywhere. I never really knew anybody who could tell you ahead of time where he was going to hit a baseball. When I get to be that kind of fool, they'll put me in a booby hatch.''

Ford Frick, then a New York sportswriter who was among Ruth's ghostwriters, also questioned the Babe. "Did you really point to the bleachers?" Frick asked. Ruth shrugged and replied, "It's in the papers, isn't it?" "Yeah," Frick said, "It's in the papers. But did you really point to the stands?" "Why don't you read it in the papers," Ruth said. "It's all right there in the papers."

Frick later became the National League president, the commissioner of all baseball. More than likely, Frick wrote *Babe Ruth's Own Book of Baseball*, published in 1928, four years before the controversial called shot. No coauthor is listed, only a notation: "By arrangement with Christy Walsh." Walsh, who had been a sporstwriter, was among the pioneer player-agents and employed a stable of ghostwriters.

Whatever, it is a remarkably good book. There is no way of knowing the extent of the Babe's participation. From my experience as a ghostwriter, I know that eventually the writer must fly solo. Assuming the Babe tired, as most athletes do, it is necessary for the ghost to go the distance. For example, on Page 274, in discussing ballplayers, Ruth offers the following observation:

People sitting in the stands . . . say, "Oh, well if he wasn't a ball player, he'd probably be digging ditches, or working on a farm" That attitude has always struck me as most unfair. You know if Galli-Curci couldn't sing she might be doing hard tasks in her native land; if Booth Tarkington couldn't write books, he might be an Indiana farmer or if Arthur Brisbane couldn't write editorials he might be a subway guard.

INTRODUCTION

This is Frick speaking, not the Babe. A native Hoosier, Frick was well-versed in opera and familiar with Tarkington's novels. He was also a Hearstling, hired by Brisbane.

Still, Frick, or whoever, should be commended. The book that resulted is instructive. What surprises me the most is how, in the seven decades since publication, there have been so few adjustments in the actual playing of the game. There are some differences, of course. In preparing for a new season, the Babe tubbed at Hot Springs, Arkansas; the players today work with weights and on the Nautilus machines.

As a writer, I am fascinated by the language of the time. Describing the well-dressed players of his day, Ruth and/or Frick says "Wait Hoyte [the Yankee pitcher] is a regular tailor's model and Clarence Rowland and Billy Evans, the umpires, were 'the glass of fashion' and the 'mould of form.' But none of them had anything on [outfielder] Duffy Lewis. He was old Kid Fashion himself."

Long-ball hitters in Ruth's time were "swing hitters," not power hitters; they swung for the fences. Ruth, of course, was the greatest "swing hitter" of his time, probably the best of all time. But there are disadvantages: more often than not they are among the league leaders in strikeouts. Because they take a longer swing, they uncoil early and are susceptible to the slow, breaking pitches.

"Some folks say I was responsible for the development of 'swing hitting,'" the Babe observed. "Maybe they're right. The minute I started hitting home runs with any frequency the newspapers took it up. The fans liked to see the ball go sailing out of the park. After the old time pitching battles, hitting of that sort was something of a novelty and a relief. Other fellows, particularly the big, burly, powerful chaps began taking their bat at the end, and 'swinging from the heels,' as the boys say. And 'swing hitting' came into prominence."

INTRODUCTION

He also explains, with some truth, why his .342 lifetime average was 25 points lower than Ty Cobb's .367 career record:

> "I'm paid to hit home runs. In a way that's a handicap. To hit home runs I've got to swing from the heels with all the power in my body. Which isn't a good batting style. And the greatest tribute I can pay to Ty Cobb is simply this: If I wasn't expected to drive the ball out of the lot every time I come up there to the plate I'd change my batting form tomorrow. I'd copy Cobb's style in every single thing he does. And I'll wager right now that if I could do that I'd increase my batting average 100 points over the season."

Ruth swung at a slight upward angle; his home runs were usually high flies that carried out of the park. Interestingly, there is no mention here of his legendary popups. No player, before or since, hit the ball so high in the air. Many infielders have told of how they had to wait "a minute or two" before they were able to corral a Ruth popup.

I am reminded of a story told by Ray Berres, a big-league catcher who later gained considerable prominence as a pitching coach:

> "I was a kid trying to break in with the Oklahoma City club, my first year as a pro. We were playing a spring exhibition with the Yankees. Bases loaded and Ruth hit a towering pop fly right above me. It was a speck in the sky. I kept tracking it but I stumbled on the mound and fell backwards. The ball hit the pitcher's rubber and bounced nine miles up. Everybody scored and the Babe wound up on second with a double."

Berres laughed at the recollection. "And I went nineteen years before I missed another one." He continued:

INTRODUCTION

"The Babe made it a point to come by me when the inning was over and told me not to let it get me down. He said he had seen it happen to a lot of seasoned, big league catchers. And several years later, when I came up with the [Brooklyn] Dodgers, we played an exhibition game in Yankee Stadium and he came by and said, 'Well, kid, I see you made it.'"

Although he seldom remembered names—everyone was "Kid"—the Babe was constantly encouraging younger players. This characteristic comes through in his book. Instruction is offered on every phase of the game: how to play the outfield and the infield, how to bunt, how and why the catcher is so important, the cut-off throw, the hit-and-run and why runs are much more crucial than hits. His advice to budding pitchers (he broke in as a pitcher) is as sound today as it was more than a half century ago:

"The first thing any pitcher has got to develop—the biggest single item in his whole stock of trade—is control! Don't let anyone kid you about it. The curve and the fast one are important; the change of pace and the other trick deliveries are great—but they're not worth a plugged nickel unless you have control to go with them.

"And by control I don't mean the ability to put the ball over the plate somewhere between the shoulders . . . I mean the ability to hit a three-inch target nine throws out of ten . . . the sort of control that lets you put the ball in the exact spot you want it, and to play a corner to the split fraction of an inch."

The Babe and Ford Frick & Co. did it for the money. But they did leave a valuable book.

CONTENTS

CHAPTER I

CONTENTS

CONTENTS

CONTENTS

xvi

CONTENTS

ILLUSTRATIONS

ILLUSTRATIONS

ILLUSTRATIONS

BABE RUTH'S OWN BOOK OF BASEBALL

BABE RUTH'S OWN BOOK OF BASEBALL

CHAPTER I

The Baltimore River front—Street corner baseball—Days at
St. Mary's—The first contract—A word of advice from
Brother Gilbert—The big leagues at last—The climb up-
ward—Aid from team-mates—A $70,000 contract—
Looking back.

My earliest recollections center about the dirty,
traffic-crowded streets of Baltimore's river front.

Crowded streets they were too, noisy with the roar
of heavy trucks whose drivers cursed and swore and
aimed blows with their driving whips, at the legs
of kids who made the streets their playground.

And the youngsters, running wild, struck back and
echoed the curses. Truck-drivers were our enemies:
so were the coppers patrolling their beats, and so too
were the shopkeepers who took bruising payment
from our skins for the apples and the fruit we
"snitched" from their stands and counters.

A rough, tough neighborhood, but I liked it.

There in those crooked winding streets I staged my first fight, and lost it, I think. There too I played my first baseball. There I learned to fear and to hate the coppers. Perhaps it was there, too, that I learned to control my pitches. For tossing over-ripe apples, or aged eggs at a truck driver's head is mighty good practice—although I don't recommend it to the boys of today.

Many people thought I was an orphan. I wasn't. My folks lived in Baltimore and my father worked in the district where I was raised. We were poor. Very poor. And there were times when we never knew where the next meal was coming from. But I never minded. I was no worse off than the other kids with whom I played and fought.

I don't know how I happened to be sent to St. Mary's school. As a matter of fact it wasn't so much a school as it was a home where kids like me could be cared for and trained and taught as they should be. All I remember is that I was a loose jointed, gangling dirty-faced kid in knee pants playing in the street, where one day a round-faced pleasant little man in clerical garb came over to talk to me.

I thought he was a priest and I called him Father, and tipped my cap when I spoke to him.

4

"Not Father," he said, smiling, "Just Brother—Brother Gilbert."

Then he told me that I was to go with him, that I would be given a fine home and taught things that would make me into a useful citizen. I didn't want to go. I liked the freedom of the street; liked the gang of youngsters I played with and prowled with.

But I went.

For a while I wasn't happy. I missed the crowds, and the dirt, and the noise of the street. I missed the other kids. I even missed the policemen and the beatings that came from the shopkeepers when we were unfortunate enough to fall into their clutches. As I look back at it now I realize that I must have been a real problem to the Brothers.

But Brother Gilbert stuck with me. I owe him a lot. More than I'll ever be able to repay.

It was Brother Gilbert who finally struck upon the thing to hold my interest and keep me happy. It was baseball. Once I had been introduced to school athletics I was satisfied and happy. Even as a kid I was big for my years, and because of my size I used to get most any job I liked on the team. Sometimes I pitched. Sometimes I caught, and frequently I played the outfield and infield. It was all the same to me. All I wanted was to play. I didn't care much where.

As I grew older, Brother Gilbert encouraged me more and more. At sixteen I had developed into a pretty good catcher and was beginning to hit pretty well. I was tall and skinny in those days, and from some of the pictures that still hang on the walls over at school I guess I must have been about as funny looking a kid as ever got a trouncing for cutting classes to go fishing.

There were a lot of fine men connected with the school in those days. In addition to Brother Gilbert, there was Brother Mathias. What a friend he was, as I found out during 1924 and 1925 when things were breaking bad and I needed friends as I never had needed them before. Then there were Brother Albin and Brother Paul—men whom I still see frequently and who never fail to send me letters of congratulation every time I do something worth while. These men are among the very few people who call me George. To the rest of the world, and particularly to the baseball fans I'm "Babe" and have been ever since I broke into baseball. To the members of the Yankee ball Club I'm "Jedge." That's a name that Benny Bengough tacked on me some two or

6

three seasons ago, and it has stuck. But to the Brothers down at St. Mary's I'm George, and always will be.

It's a funny thing, incidentally, how many times a year I get letters asking me how I got my nickname. Some of the newspaper boys made a pretty good yarn out of it one time. They said that when I was a little kid I always wanted to play ball with bigger boys, and when they wouldn't let me play I'd cry and howl until I had the whole neighborhood disturbed. The big boys, according to his story, nicknamed me "Baby" because I cried so much, then shortened it to Babe, as kids will.

It's a shame to spoil a good yarn like that, but as a matter of fact the story is all wrong. A man named Steinam, who was coach of the Baltimore Orioles when I joined the club in 1914, gave me the nickname. The first day I reported at the clubhouse he said, "Well, here's Jack's newest Babe now."

And the name has stuck. I've been "Babe" ever since and I suppose I will still be "Babe" when I'm an old, old man with wobbly legs and long whiskers. They tell another story about the way I happened to get into league baseball, too. According to some of the newspaper men, the brothers at school tried me out at everything in the world. They had me doing work in the garden, and they tried me out at carpentry. They had me try bookkeeping for a while, and about everything else they could think of. But I couldn't seem to get the hang of any of them. Finally (and don't forget this is a newspaper yarn and not a confession) Brother Gilbert sent for Jack Dunn, owner and manager of the Baltimore club. Dunn came over and according to the story Brother Gilbert got him off to one side and said:

"Jack, I've got a young fellow here that I want you to look over. I don't know that he's a ball player, but I'm sure he must be. They say every boy can do something well and I've tried this youngster at everything else. It must be he's a ball player."

True or not, you've got to admit it's a good story.

As a matter of fact Brother Gilbert was responsible for me getting a chance. He used to coach our baseball team, and he liked the way I did things. Lots of times he would point me out as an example to the other boys, as a baseball player you understand, and finally, when I was eighteen he wrote a letter to Jack Dunn telling him about me and asking Jack to come around and see for himself.

THE FIRST CONTRACT

Now baseball managers don't usually look for prospective players on schoolboy teams. And I imagine if St. Mary's hadn't been convenient and handy Jack wouldn't have paid any attention to the letter. But it was only a few steps from his office to the school and he had nothing else to do so he came over.

I'll never forget the day Brother Gilbert called me over and introduced me to Jack. I was flabbergasted. I hadn't known about the letter and the idea of shaking hands with a real professional baseball man was almost too much. Jack was mighty good to me and talked for quite a while about baseball. Finally he got me into a uniform and out in the yard. He had me pitch to him for a half hour I guess, talking to me all the time, and telling me not to strain and not to try too hard. I was a pretty fair pitcher in those days if I do say so myself, and at the end of a half hour Dunn called a halt and went into the office with Brother Gilbert.

In about a half hour they called me in and Brother Gilbert explained that Mr. Dunn thought I would make a ball player and wanted me to sign a contract with the Baltimore Orioles. Since I wasn't yet of age, Brother Gilbert explained, Mr. Dunn would

9

take out papers as my guardian and would be responsible for me when I was away from the school.

"How about it young man," Dunn asked me, "do you want to play baseball?"

I guess I must have come near falling over in my excitement. Did I want to play baseball? Does a fish like to swim or a squirrel climb trees?

I didn't even pause to ask questions.

"Sure," I said, "I'll play. When do I start?"

But Brother Gilbert stopped me.

"Wait a minute, George," he said, "this is a serious business. Boys play baseball for fun, but you're a man now and you're taking a man's job. You know playing professional baseball isn't like playing on the sandlots. You'll find the men on the Baltimore team know a lot more baseball than you do. And it won't be easy. Besides," he added, "I want you to understand all the arrangements. Mr. Dunn has agreed to pay you $600 for the six-months season. That's approximately $25 a week. Will you be satisfied with that?"

Looking back now of course, six hundred dollars doesn't look like much money. But that day, there in the school office, it sounded like a fortune. And twenty-five dollars a week! Why I'd be as rich as

Rockefeller, I thought. And for playing baseball!
I never even hesitated. If Brother Gilbert expected
me to do any serious thinking he certainly got a disappointment that day.

"Sure, I'd like it," I said, and said it fast too, for
fear Dunn might change his mind. And so it was
arranged. A contract was drawn up, and I signed it.
Then I beat it out of doors to tell the rest of the boys.

In the years that have gone by I've had a lot of
thrills. I got one when I pitched my first world series
game. I get one every time I hit a ball over the
fence and I got a big one that day last fall when I
hit my sixtieth home run and broke my old record.
But none of these could compare to the thrill that
came the day I paraded out to the playground
and told the rest of the boys that I was signed to a
contract—a real, honest-to-goodness professional
baseball player!

Less than two years ago I sat in Colonel Ruppert's
private office in New York and signed my name
again—this time to a three year contract calling for
$70,000 a year. The newspaper boys were on hand,
and the photographers, and the whole baseball world
made a great ado about this signing. But honestly,
that new contract for the largest salary ever paid a

ball player didn't give me half the kick I got that afternoon back in 1914 when I signed with Jack Dunn to play ball with the Baltimore Orioles at $25 a week.

Speaking of that last contract signing, reminds me of a good laugh I had at the expense of the newspaper boys. There were a couple of dozen of them sticking around when I signed, some of them fellows who had been traveling with the Yankees for several seasons; fellows whom I know intimately and well. Yet in their stories, every one of them wrote about me signing that contract with my left hand and some of the papers even ran pictures showing me signing left-handed!

How they managed it I don't know—for as a matter of fact I write with my right hand now, and I always have. I'm left-handed in everything else I do, but when it comes to writing I'm just as right-handed as any right-hander you ever saw. It just goes to show that people take a lot of things for granted. They don't observe things closely, particularly things about which they feel confident.

Most of the rest of my story everyone knows.

I went with the Orioles and was fortunate enough to make good. In fact I never for a moment thought that I wouldn't. I don't believe I was cocky and I don't believe I was any fresher than the average rookie who gets a chance to sign a contract—but I was confident.

I played for Jack Dunn for a month and at the end of that time he raised my contract six hundred dollars more, just doubling the original amount. At the end of the second month he added another six hundred. And right here let me say one thing. I've heard a lot of talk and read a lot of stuff in the newspapers about club owners being tightwads and all that sort of thing. If they are I have never discovered it. In my baseball experience I've found them fair at all times, always willing to pay a man what they considered he was worth. Never in my life have I ever been a serious hold-out, and never have I had any very bitter salary arguments with my owners.

Of course Colonel Ruppert may be an exception. Many people tell me he is. And he is the only man I've had to do business with since I've been in the big-money class. But he certainly has been fair and square always, in all his dealings with me. The tip-off on that is the fact that it took us less than twenty minutes to agree to terms in 1927, when I signed my last contract.

In 1914 Jack Dunn sold me to the Boston Red Sox. I was in the big leagues sure enough.

I've never been back to the minors since. In 1914, after I reported to the Red Sox I got into four ball games. Not many, but a start, at least. The next year I was in forty-two. Since then I've never been in less.

Going to the Red Sox was a great break. In those days the Red Sox were as much kings of the baseball walk as the Yankees are today. Then I was on the same club with Bill Carrigan, one of the finest chaps I ever knew, and one of the best coaches of young pitchers there is in the game. With the Red Sox I really began to learn a little baseball. We had a great pitching staff in those days. Joe Wood, Dutch Leonard, Ernie Shore, Hugh Bedient, George Foster—what an array that was! And chaps, all of them, who not only know how to pitch themselves, but fellows who could teach others as well. Joe Wood was so good as an instructor, in fact, that he's still at it—coaching baseball up at Yale where I see him quite often.

A young fellow couldn't have been with a better outfit to learn the game. While I didn't realize it at the time, I was learning some real baseball from two other fellows on the club, too; learning lessons that were to help me a whole lot later on. These two were Harry Hooper and Tris Speaker. I've always maintained, and I still believe, that Harry Hooper was one of the greatest outfielders who ever lived. As a defensive player I believe he rated even higher than Tris Speaker, and that's going-some. It was from these two that I learned a lot about playing the outfield, and it was their coaching and their example which made it easy for me to switch to the outfield later on when I joined the New York club.

In the Red Sox days I didn't think much of becoming a slugger. I liked to hit. All fellows do. There isn't a man in baseball today who isn't happiest when he's up there at the plate with a stick in his hand. But it was pitching which took my time in Boston. And one of the proudest records I hold to this day is that of having pitched the most consecutive scoreless innings in world series play.

And another accomplishment of those Boston pitching days which still makes me grin every time I think of it, occurred in a game I pitched in Detroit. In that game, in the ninth inning with nobody out and the Red Sox holding a one-run lead, I struck out Bob Veach, Ty Cobb and Sam Crawford in a row. No home run in the world ever brought a greater kick than that.

As to my home run hitting—well, I suppose I get a hundred letters a season asking me about my first home run. To tell the honest truth I don't remember exactly when I made it, or who was pitching at the time. I suppose it's all written down in the records somewhere, but I'm honest when I say I don't remember. I know it was sometime in 1915.

During my playing days in Boston I made a lot of friends and liked the place a lot. When I was sold to New York I left with a great deal of real regret. Even now when I go back to Boston for a series it's just like going home. I don't believe I have any more real friends any where, or any more boosters, than I have up there at Fenway Park where I started my big league career.

I went to New York in 1920 and I've been there ever since. I hope I can remain there and finish my big league career with the Yankees. New York has been mighty good to me. Like all young fellows, I've made mistakes. Several times I've got away on the wrong foot. Once or twice I've been in bad with the baseball authorities. I've figured in rows with

THE BABE CONNECTS FOR A HOME RUN IN THE THIRD GAME OF THE 1927 WORLD SERIES. EARL SMITH SHOWN BEHIND THE BAT FOR THE PIRATES. THE PITTSBURG PLAYERS CAN BE SEEN IN THE DUGOUT, WITH BOB MEUSEL SWINGING A BAT IN THE FOREGROUND. SQUATTED DOWN ALONG THE LINE IS EDDIE BENNETT, YANKEE MASCOT

THERE IT GOES! RUTH CAUGHT BY THE CAMERA JUST AS HE HITS ONE. NOTICE HOW HIS SWING PULLS HIS BODY AROUND IN PERFECT POSITION TO START THE DASH TO FIRST BASE. PICTURE TAKEN IN 1923 WORLD SERIES. HANK GOWDY CATCHING

the umpires and fights with fans. But those days are over. I know better now.

Tommy Connolly, the umpire, and I hold one joint record. The last time Tommy was forced to kick a player out of the ball game was back in 1922. I was the player. Tommy has had a clean record since that day. So have I. That's the last time I have had a serious run-in with an umpire.

During the years that I've been in the big leagues, stories have been printed about me that were complimentary—and a lot of things have been said which weren't exactly compliments. I've had my ups and my downs, and there have been times when it looked as though my baseball career was over and finished. In 1925 when I collapsed in Asheville, during the spring training trip, a lot of people figured I'd never put on a uniform again. That sickness taught me a lesson. It was my own fault. I took life easy all winter, put on a lot of fat and overweight, then tried to boil and fast myself into shape in a couple of weeks. It can't be done.

All through the years though, from first to last, I've had one lot of friends who have stuck by me. That's the kids.

I'm proud of my record in baseball, and I'd be un-

17

grateful to say otherwise. Every time I drive in a run, every time I hit a ball over the fence or hear the cheers of the bleacher fans ringing in my ears I get a great kick. I suppose I always will.

The first year I broke into baseball I got one fan letter—and that one was from Brother Gilbert.

Last year there were 20,000 letters in my mail, from every part of the globe and every state in the Union. I had a letter from a Brahman priest in India, and I had a letter from a condemned man in a Cuban jail. I had a letter from an eight year old boy in Germany and another from a college professor in Japan.

To answer them all would be impossible. But I like to get them. Seems to me as though they're part of my pay. But I'm not kidding myself. The "razzberries" are just as easy to collect as the cheers. The people who cheer me from the stands or write me letters aren't interested so much in Babe Ruth as they are in something else. They're interested in baseball.

All ball players realize that sooner or later.

What a game it is!

No wonder a fellow gets a kick out of being in it and part of it. No wonder we're proud, all of us, to be ball players!

CHAPTER II

You know a game of baseball is like a battle. One
outfit digs in behind the barb wire of good pitching
and great fielding and the other side tries to shell
them loose with a barrage of base hits. Just like
war, it's a battle of defense against offense and the
best organization wins.

If you happen to be a baseball fan who reads the
newspapers you've probably noticed that before a
world series or any other big series the writers always print long stories of comparisons between individual players. They point out that Lou Gehrig,
for instance, will hit a ball further and harder than
Joe Harris, but that Pie Traynor can go farther to
his left than Joe Dugan. That's interesting—but

so far as doping out the winner of the series is concerned, its bunk. And it always gives the ball players a laugh.

For ball players know that it isn't individuals who count. It's the way a team plays as a whole, that determines its offensive power or its defensive strength. Smart ball players and smart managers consider offense and defense as units knowing that it takes nine men to do the fielding and nine hitters to make up a batting order that will score runs.

That's where Miller Huggins is a smart guy. Hug doesn't worry about the other fellow, and he won't let his players worry. Before we went into the world series last fall the boys were sitting around the clubhouse punching the bag and "barbering" a little about what we might expect in the series.

Shawkey and Shocker and Pennock had been discussing the Pirate hitters and how to pitch to them when Mark Koenig broke into the conversation. Mark is a nervous, high strung fellow who takes his baseball mighty seriously.

"I guess this Wright is quite a whiz," he remarked. "They tell me he can go a lot further after a ball than I can. And Traynor is getting a lot of play too at third. I wonder if Joe and I will be able to hold our own with them." Hug overheard him.

"Listen," Hug said, and it was one of the smartest remarks I ever heard. "You fellows don't need to worry about the Pirates. In baseball all a fellow has to do to win is to drive in a few runs and then field well enough to keep the other fellow from scoring as many. I'm not a darn bit interested in whether Wright is a better shortstop than you are, Mark, or whether Lou or Tony are better men than they have. We've got just nine men to play the nine positions. Good or bad, they're the ones who have to do the job and all the worry about the other fellow don't help a bit. Our job is to make the most of what we have and the Pirates be durned."

Now, if you know a better philosophy for baseball than that, go to it! I don't.

The ideal baseball team, of course, would be one that was equally good on defense and offense and perfect in both departments. But teams like that don't exist. And my experience has been that the team which is particularly strong offensively is apt to be a little weak on defense and vice versa. It's up to the manager or the Captain to make the most of what he has in the way of material, and he naturally builds up the department in which he is strongest even if he has to weaken the other department a bit to do it.

Baseball has changed a lot in the last ten or fifteen years. I haven't been sticking around the big leagues as long as Ty Cobb and Eddie Collins and some of those fellows, but I've been around long enough to notice the change. And it hasn't been in one club or two clubs either, but in the whole game.

When I first broke in baseball was a defensive game. The pitchers and fielders had all the best of the argument, and a two run lead could be cashed in most any time.

What an array of pitchers there was in those days! Walter Johnson was in his prime then, and Alexander, and Rube Marquard and Eddie Plank. And those boys could pitch, believe me. They had everything it takes to make a great pitcher, and in addition they were permitted to rough the ball, use trick deliveries and do anything else they could think of to make a hitter's life miserable. And besides that the ball they used in those days was dead into the bargain.

I guess that period is what you would call baseball's defensive age.

And naturally with the big leagues playing defensive ball the sand lotters and the amateurs took it up too. Kids in those days dreamed of becoming great pitchers and hitting was just a matter of course. Even hitters like Wagner and Lajoie had to play second fiddle to the Mattys and the Browns, and though a fellow like Cobb might be a marvel, folks kept their eyes on the pitchers.

Even now before a world series you find a lot of the experts predicting that "pitching will win the series." And, all other things being equal it will. But the fact is that the statement is a throw back to the old defensive age when pitching was the big thing in baseball and everything else could run for Sweeney.

The change from defensive to offensive play came gradually. John McGraw was one of the men who was most responsible. There's one cagey hombre, that McGraw. He's always just a couple of jumps ahead of the other fellow when it comes to thinking, and he's always looking for something new and unusual to pull. I've had my run-ins with John and once or twice when we were playing the Giants in the world series I've wanted to sock him in the nose, but he's a baseball wizard just the same.

And while all the other managers were going nutty over defensive play and making themselves bald trying to dope out ways to develop and aid their pitchers, John took counsel with himself and decided that what baseball needed was more action. So he went in for hitting and base-stealing, and the first thing the rest of the managers knew John was stealing a pennant right out of their laps.

While other fellows were content to string along with the old fashioned sacrifice with a man on base, John took a gambling chance with the hit and run, and the steal. Instead of sending hitters up to the plate with orders to "Wait 'em out," John would pat a fellow on the back and say: "Go up there and lay on that onion. Knock it a mile. You're better than he is."

And how the fans liked it!

They had been watching pitching perfection for so long that they craved a change, and given a taste, they began to yell for more hitting and more action.

Other managers began to copy McGraw's style, too, and it wasn't long before they passed rules limiting pitchers on trick stuff. They did away with the spit ball and the emery ball and the other freaks. They built a little more life into the ball and they ordered umpires to use new and clean balls as much as possible.

The boys began smacking the fences with long drives, outfielders began playing with their backs to the wall and infielders had to move back on the grass or have their legs torn off with hot drives. And that's the story of how baseball's era of defensive play passed into history and offensive play became the main factor in the game. At least that's the way it seems to me—and most of the changes have taken place since I first put on a big league uniform.

Right here, too, let me say that I've been a pretty lucky fellow in that respect. In the old days when defense was the big thing, I was a pitcher and a pretty good one if I do say it myself. And when things switched over and hitting became the rage Ed Barrow, then managing the Red Sox, turned me into an outfielder and gave me a chance to "take my cut" with the rest of the sluggers. So I got a break going and coming. You can't beat that!

A lot of folks, and particularly the older fans,

still think that the old style was best, and they sit around and pine for the good old days when "Pitchers were pitchers instead of throwers," and teams had to fight for one run instead of "getting 'em in clusters."

Maybe they're right. I'm not arguing the matter one way or another. I'm just trying to point out that baseball, as a game, can be divided into two big departments. One is defensive play. That's the business of stopping the other fellow, and it includes pitching, fielding, throwing and the inside strategy that makes two putouts where one grew before. The other is offensive play and that's simply the matter of your own attack—hitting, base-running, stealing, etc.—the business of *scoring runs.*

Both departments are necessary. And baseball strategy, when you come down to it, is simply making the most of your strength in these two departments.

Right now the fans demand emphasis on offensive play. And what the fans want they get. They like plenty of hitting—so modern baseball is built around the slugger. Some day perhaps public sentiment will switch back the other way, back again to the old days of pitching battles and low scores. If it does you'll see a return to the old style in a hurry and there will be new Mathewsons and new Browns springing up to take the place of the Speakers, the Cobbs, the Gehrigs and the Hornsbys of the present slugging era.

As concerns the fine points of the two styles, there's plenty of room for argument. Managers build their ball clubs from the material they have available. If they have too much defensive strength, then they have to make defense their specialty. If, on the other hand, they have plenty of offensive power, then they must build such a club and make their defense a secondary thing.

But to get back once more to cases instead of generalities. Take the time to go over the baseball records and you'll find the great teams of history excelled in one department or the other. They can be classified either as defensive teams or offensive teams.

The greatest defensive team of all time, I guess, was the Chicago White Sox of 1906. Those boys hit so little that whenever a player got a two-bagger he wrote home about it, and if they got more than four hits in a game Commy threw a banquet in their honor. But just the same they won a pennant and a world series, and the reason they won was that they were so good defensively that they managed to hold the other fellows to even fewer runs than they got.

They had great pitching. I never saw them, but the old boys are still talking about Ed Walsh, Frank Smith, Doc White, Nick Altrock and the rest of that famous outfit. And along with their pitching they had wonderful fielding strength plus baseball brains. And brains is one of the biggest assets in defensive play. A fellow can stand up there at the plate and take his cut without any deep thinking, but to play the field properly a fellow has to have something besides curly hair above his shoulders. He's got to know his onions.

The old Athletics were another great defensive team, too. I've played against them and I know. But coming as they did, at the time when baseball was changing—they had real offensive strength too. Just the same it was the fine pitching of fellows like Combs and Bender and Plank, plus the high class work of that million-dollar infield that made them one of the greatest teams of all time. Despite the swatting power of Baker, McInnis, Collins and the rest I still figure that they class as a defensive rather than an offensive team. Among modern teams, the Washington Senators of 1924 rate as one of the best defensive teams, combining fine pitching with some corking work in the infield and outfield. You'll go far and look plenty before you'll find a better infield combination than Bucky Harris and Roger Peckinpaugh put up that year, for instance.

When it comes to great offensive teams I'm just cocky enough to believe that the Yankees of 1927 were the best ever. Believe me that outfit of ours could hit and score runs. The records tell the story —and there are mighty few hitting records that we didn't shatter to bits.

Incidentally there's another place where I've had to argue with my good friend John McGraw. John maintains that the old Baltimore Orioles were one of the great offensive clubs. And he rather has me there. John saw both the Orioles and the 1927 Yankees while I wasn't taking much interest in baseball at the time the Orioles were good. Under the circumstances I'll have to take his word for it— but I'll never admit that the Orioles packed a greater wallop than the Yankees last year. I don't think it's possible.

The Detroit Tigers, winners of the American League pennant in 1907, 1908 and 1909, were a great offensive club. They had Cobb and Crawford and McIntyre and Jones and big Schmidt—all of them hitters. And as an offensive club they stood out in an age when defensive play was considered quite the thing. Real hitters those fellows, and they have proved it during the years that have followed, with the now-bald Tyrus still able to stand up there at the plate and hit with the best of them, despite the weight of more than 22 years of baseball activity.

Discussion of great offensive teams would not be complete without some mention of the 1912-1913 Giants—the team that was responsible for the gradual swing from defensive to offensive play. There was a team that was great offensively, not so much on account of its hitting power, but because of its cleverness in base-running. Old-timers still maintain that the Giants team of that era literally "stole" the pennant. They were masters at base running in an age when base running was a real art.

Perhaps I've rambled a bit through these pages. The point I want to make and leave strong is simply this. Baseball, as a game, is divided into two great divisions. One is offense, the other is defense. They are equally important, but in building up a ball club it is very seldom, indeed, that you can find men equally proficient in each department. Consequently most managers determine in which department they are best, and they make their playing plans along that line—weakening one department a little perhaps, in order to strengthen the other.

And at the present time baseball is going through an offensive era with hitters holding the edge and the science of steal and sacrifice playing second fiddle to brawn and power and wallop.

CHAPTER III

PITCHING is the most important single item in the defensive play of any ball club. But I mean real pitching, not just throwing. I guess there isn't a kid in the country but at some time or another dreams of being a great pitcher. And here's the first thing for him to remember.

Pitchers—real pitchers—learn early that their job isn't so much to keep opposing batsmen from hitting as it is to make them hit at someone. The trouble with most kid pitchers is that they forget there are eight other men on the team to help them. They just blunder ahead, putting everything they have on every pitch, and trying to carry the weight of the whole game on their shoulders. The result is that they tire out and go bad along in the middle of the game, and then the wise old heads have to hurry out and rescue them.

I've seen a lot of young fellows come up, and they all had the same trouble. Take Lefty Grove over at Philadelphia, for instance. There isn't a pitcher in the league who has more speed or more stuff than Lefty. He can do things with a baseball that make you dizzy. But when he first came into the league he seemed to think that he had to strike every batter out as he came up. The result was that he'd go along great for five or six innings, and then blow. And he's just now learning to conserve his strength. In other words, he's learning that a little exercise of the noodle will save a lot of wear and tear on his arm.

Owen Carroll, the Holy Cross star, who went to the Tigers, is another of the same type. Ownie was a whiz in college, but when he got up into the big show he found out that there was something more to pitching than just breezing that fast one past. It took him a whole season to get wise, and he is just now beginning to develop as a real pitcher. He's getting smart.

You see when a kid pitcher starts out he tries to

carry the game himself. Then when he finds out that he's being hit a little he tries to bear down harder and harder. And the more he bears down the worse he gets.

I broke in as a pitcher and I was like all the rest of the beginners. And I couldn't understand why that fast ball didn't fool the big league hitters like it had the kids back at school. I had another bad fault, too. I wouldn't accept advice and how I managed to blunder along is more than I can understand.

The boys are still telling a story about me that always gets a laugh even if it isn't very complimentary. In the 1918 world series we (the Boston Red Sox) were playing the Chicago Cubs, and they had Leslie Mann and Max Flack alternating in the outfield.

I was slated to pitch one game and the first time up Mann socked me for a base hit. When I went back to the bench Bill Carrigan, our manager, called me over to give me some advice.

"That fellow Mann is a tough hitter against left handed pitching," Bill said. "The only thing to do is loosen him up a bit. The next time he comes up to hit dust him off! Drop him in the dirt! Maybe that will stop him!"

CONTROL AS A PITCHING FACTOR

I promised Bill I would do it, and went on about my business.

Meantime the Cubs had sent Flack in to replace Mann, and when Max came up to hit I promptly turned loose a fast one that flattened him.

When I went back to the bench I was feeling pretty proud of myself.

"Well," I said, "I guess I showed that guy Mann a thing or two, didn't I?"

I thought Carrigan would explode. He cussed me up one side and down the other. And I don't blame him. Can you imagine a pitcher not even knowing the difference between hitters and hitting Max Flack in the ribs thinking all the time that he was making Leslie Mann a victim?

But it just goes to show how careless young pitchers can be, and it's typical too of the thousand and one things which inexperienced pitchers will do to get in bad.

The first thing any pitcher has got to develop— the biggest single item in his whole stock of trade— is control! Don't let anyone kid you about it. The curve and the fast one are important; the change of pace and the other trick deliveries are great—but they're not worth a plugged nickle unless you have control to go with them.

And by control I don't mean the ability to put the ball over the plate somewhere between the shoulders and the knees, either. I mean the ability to hit a three inch target nine throws out of ten. I mean the sort of control that lets you put that ball in the exact spot you want it, and to play a corner to the split fraction of an inch.

I've seen a lot of good pitchers in my day. That gang I broke in with up in Boston was a pretty fair outfit. And there wasn't a man in the lot who didn't spend hours on end getting control. Ernie Shore could just about drive a nail at sixty feet and Dutch Leonard was just as good. When they pitched they didn't guess where that ball was going. They knew.

In the 1926 world series when Alexander struck out Tony Lazzeri in that crucial inning and won a championship a lot of fellows raved about Alex's great curves. Let me tell you a little secret. Alex threw Tony just one curve ball in all those pitches. And the ball that Tony fanned on wasn't a curve at all. It wasn't even a fast one. It was a half-speed ball that cut the corner of the plate within a half inch of the spot Bob O'Farrell called for.

ALEXANDER THE OLD MASTER

No sir, the thing that fanned Tony Lazzeri that day and the thing that cost the Yankees a world championship was Grover Alexander's uncanny control. He was putting that ball right where he wanted it, on every pitch. And the fellow who was up there at the plate with a bat on his shoulder felt like a sucker. For he knew that the balls were so bad he couldn't hit them squarely, yet they were good enough that they were sure to be called strikes if he let them go.

I know. I stood up there. And I felt like a sucker along with the rest of the boys.

Of course there aren't many pitchers who have the control that Alex has. Alex is a tall, loose-jointed easy-going chap who refuses to become excited. Just to see Old Pete out there on the mound with that cocky little, undersized cap pulled down over one ear, chewing away at his tobacco and pitching baseballs as easy as pitching hay, is enough to take the heart out of a fellow. I've got a hunch that if Alex suddenly found himself on the moon, he'd just grin, pull his cap over his ear, and keep on chewing. He's that kind of a chap. Nothing rattles him.

Urban Shocker is another one who makes good

control take the place of a lot of other things. Shocker is a mighty smart hombre out there on the mound, believe me. Time was when he used to have a good assortment of "stuff" too—but now, as he gets older, he's losing a lot of the "swift." And his "hook" doesn't break any more, it just bends a little.

But Shocker has got two things that most amateur pitchers lack. He has control—and he's got a lot of knowledge up there under that old baseball cap of his. And the two get him over many a rough, tough spot, believe me.

As I said, the first thing any pitcher has to get to become something besides a "thrower" is control.

And there's just one way to get it—that's by constant practice. Some day when you're out at the ball park during fielding practice, watch the pitchers warming up. You'll see them all out there playing toss, old timers and youngsters alike. But if you watch closely you'll see one big difference.

The young fellows are just throwing—loosening up their arms and getting the kinks out of their muscles. But the old fellows! They're pitching to a target with every ball they throw! Watch the fellow who is warming them up. You'll see him hold his glove up as a target on every pitch. Sometimes he holds it over one corner of the plate, sometimes over the other. Sometimes he holds it low and sometimes high. But always the pitcher is in there trying to hit the mark—and if he happens to be on form he'll do it twenty-nine pitches out of thirty. If he can't, then he's still a long way from a pitcher.

I've seen Shawkey pitch to a target for an hour at a time, perfecting his control. He doesn't pitch hard, and he doesn't strain his arm with a lot of "stuff." He just pitches away at that old mark. And other players on the club do the same thing. Our fellows, most of them, are veterans. They've been around. They know what it's all about. And they know just how important control is.

Walter Johnson is another pitcher who was great on control. He had to be. If Walter had been wild with that fast ball of his, a hitter wouldn't have dared to stand up there. It would have been murder. But you never heard fellows complain about hitting against Walter.

You might not be able to see them, and he might make you look like a sucker when he sent that fast ball whizzing past your shoulders like a bullet. But always you could dig in there at the plate knowing deep in your gizzard that whatever else happened, he wouldn't "bean" you. For every time he pitched he knew right where that ball was going. He had to. If he had been inclined to wildness with all that speed, there isn't a catcher in the business could have caught him.

Believe me the catchers are the fellows who suffer when a pitcher is wild. In one game down South last year, when Hug was trying out his young pitchers, Johnny Grabowski was so bruised and battered that he had to take a four day rest. Those kids had him diving in the dirt and jumping in the air. They had him running to the right and hopping to left and when the game was finished he had big blue bruises up and down both shins, on his arms and in about every other spot on his anatomy that didn't happen to be covered with pads. Believe me, Johnny is one boy who knows the importance of control all right.

Yet some other pitchers, like Matty or Coombs, or Herb Pennock—fellows who have a lot more "stuff" on the ball than any youngster—are what the catchers call "rocking chair pitchers." Which means that their control is so good that you could sit in a rocking chair and catch them.

To be a good pitcher you've got to have a lot of

things. You've got to have a fast ball with a "hop." You've got to have a good curve to mix in with the fast one to make it effective. You've got to have a change of pace—for it takes a change of pace to throw a batter off balance and keep him from peppering that curve or fast one against the wall.

Then you've got to have pitching knowledge—the sort of knowledge that comes from experience, and study and hard work. It takes more than a sturdy pair of shoulders to get by in the big leagues these days.

But first you've got to have control, for that's the A, B, and C in the pitcher's alphabet. The greatest curve ball in the world isn't worth a thin dime if you don't know what to do with it. The "swift" of Walter Johnson would be worthless to a chap who couldn't get the ball over the plate.

Control, that's the system

And control isn't a gift that is born to a man. It's the result of hard, hard work and long hours of practice.

And in striving for control there are these things to remember. First of all you've got to develop a smooth, easy, pitching motion. Overhand, side arm or underhand it doesn't make any difference. The best one is the one that is easiest and most natural.

And you can't afford to strain. The moment a pitcher starts to strain—"bearing down" we call it in baseball—he becomes wild. The first rule of golf which says "make your swing easy and natural, and don't press," could well be named as the first rule in pitching, too.

After that one's mastered there's time enough to start work on the other details of curve and fast one.

After all, the whole thing can be summed up in a little story of an incident that happened in training camp two years ago. Hug had a lot of young pitchers in camp that year and he appointed Bob Shawkey as a sort of advisory coach.

The kids were all anxious to make good and the minute Bob would show up they'd start calling him to watch their curves or take a look at their trick stuff.

Bob stood it awhile without comment.

Finally he called the gang together.

"Now listen, you fellows," he said, "I've looked at curved balls until I'm cockeyed and I've watched fast ones until my eyeballs ache. Now you fellows line up there and try throwing at that backstop. After you've learned to hit that we'll put up a barrel and maybe in a week or two some of you will get good enough to throw a ball over the plate.

"When you get that good, then I'll be glad to talk to you about pitching. Until then I'm too busy to be bothered."

Which may sound a little hard boiled, but if you were a baseball man you'd understand. Shawkey wasn't talking through his hat at all. He just knew his onions, that's all.

CHAPTER IV

ONE day last summer I happened to be standing by the news stand in the hotel lobby in Detroit when Urban Shocker came along.

He stopped to kid with me a bit, then turned to the attendant.

"Got any Chicago papers?" he asked.

The attendant handed him two papers.

"That all you got?" Shock persisted.

The attendant pulled out three or four more and finally furnished a complete set of all the morning and evening sheets for the day.

Shocker took them, then asked for Cleveland papers as well. He got these too, bought a cigar, and walked toward the elevator with a stack of papers under his arm that would choke a horse.

The news stand man watched him curiously, and

44

turned to me when Shocker finally had disappeared.

"There's a funny guy," he commented. "Every day that egg is in town he comes over and buys newspapers from other towns. And he doesn't want just one—he wants 'em all. Wonder what he does with 'em?"

"Maybe he's saving them to paper his garage," I suggested, and the news stand man laughed and forgot.

As a matter of fact I knew all the time what Shock had wanted of the papers. So did the other fellows on the club. Fellows who travel around together on a ball club year after year get to understand each other pretty well. You know each other's little peculiarities too, and after a while you learn to know just about what a chap thinks or does or believes. Ever since Shocker joined the Yankees he has been known as a "newspaper hound," and he's gradually getting the other pitchers the same way.

For Shocker wanted those newspapers for a definite reason. He bought them for a purpose, and this is it.

Every one of those papers have sports pages which Shock studies carefully. In Detroit he bought Chicago and Cleveland papers because these were the towns where we were to play next, and the box scores of the teams in those towns told him a story. Day after day he pores over the box scores and newspaper accounts like a school kid over a lesson.

He notices which men on the opposing lineup are hitting and which ones are in a slump. He notes how they go against opposing pitchers—and being a veteran and well acquainted with the styles and types of the various pitchers, he can then get a pretty good line on what sort of pitching they are hitting.

Here's the way he works.

Suppose we're playing Cleveland in a day or two. Now everyone knows that ordinarily George Burns and Joey Sewell are dangerous hitters, and that Rube Lutzke and some of the other boys are not so hot with the stick. But Shocker, studying the box scores day after day, comes around the clubhouse with a different report.

"Well," he'll say, "I notice that Burns went hitless against Zachary the other day. Up three times for a horse-collar. Guess George is having a tough time with slow balls these days." (Zachary, we all know, is a slow ball pitcher.) Quinn beat him too a week ago. Maybe we better try George out on slow ones this trip."

Or perhaps he'll call attention to the fact that Rube Lutzke, normally a weak hitter, is having a spurt and is getting a lot of basehits. Perhaps he'll come up with information that Luke Sewell (usually a corking thrower) has been a bit wild on his throws to second base for a few days or it may be some other trick information that he gleaned from the box scores.

But it's all mighty valuable in the daily business of winning ball games.

The point of course is that to become a good pitcher a man must make a close study of opposing batsmen—and Shocker is one of the closest students you'll find in the game today. Pitching after all, is about one-third arm work and two-thirds head work and the fellows who stick around longest are the pitchers who let their head take over the burden as much as possible.

Year after year you see pitchers like Alex and Jess Haines and George Uhle and Dutch Ruether and Shocker out there winning ball games. You don't think they still have the fast breaking curve and the hop on their fast one that they once had, do you? No sir! They're getting by on knowledge, making their experience and their observation pay dividends.

Good pitchers realize that every hitter who steps up there at the plate has a "groove." That's a particular spot where he likes to see the ball come. And the pitcher who pitches down the groove—"Down his alley" the boys say sometimes—is inviting trouble.

But every batter up there at the plate, no matter who he may be, has a weakness too. It may be a fast ball inside or a curve ball low and outside. It may be anyone of a dozen different things, but the point is that somewhere there's a weak spot, and the good pitcher is always looking for it.

Herb Pennock is another smart pitcher and one day, riding along on the train, I heard him explain his pitching theory to a lot of young fellows. It was short and simple, but it was 100 percent correct.

"Get that first one over the plate," Herb advised. "Then after that, make the hitter swing at his weakness and your own strength!"

What Herb meant was simply this. Every pitcher has one particular ball that he can pitch a little better than anything else in his assortment. Herb's best

BABE RUTH THE PITCHER! PHOTO SHOWS BABE AS A MEMBER
OF THE BOSTON RED SOX. NOTE THE EASY STRIDE, LOOSE MOTION
AND PERFECT PITCHING FORM AS HE LETS THE BALL GO

THE OLD MASTER WALTER JOHNSON, ONE OF THE GREATEST
PITCHERS WHO EVER LIVED. JOHNSON IS SHOWN HERE JUST AS HE
DELIVERS HIS FAST BALL. NOTICE PERFECT BALANCE AND EASE
OF MOTION

ball, for instance, is an overhand curve that swishes up to the plate and breaks down and out. Hoyt's best pitch, on the other hand is a fast ball. If you know anything about fast balls you know that they hop as they reach the batter. Hoyt's fast one is a little different. It doesn't hop, it jumps—that is it rises, and as a result is particularly effective.

Now the point is this. You watch Hoyt and Herb when they're pitching and get a batter in the hole where he has to hit. Suppose he has two strikes and one ball for instance: or a three and two count. Or suppose the hit and run is on and the pitcher knows that the batter is going to hit the next one. Right there you'll see Herb coming in with that overhand curve or Waite with his fast one. In other words as long as the hitter is going to swing, and they know it, they'll see to it that he's swinging at the best they have and not at a cripple. That's good pitching judgment.

And by reason of good control they send that "best bet" zipping along to the batter's weakness— inside, outside, high or low as the case may be.

Of course there are a few hitters like Cobb and Hornsby who have no real weakness. They hit anything, anywhere. One of the best laughs ever

49

enjoyed in baseball was brought about by the young pitcher who walked into the clubhouse one day and announced very seriously that he had been studying the situation and at last had discovered Ty Cobb's weakness.

"Boy, if you have you're a wonder," one of the veterans said. "What do you think it is?"

"Well," the rookie replied, "so near as I can figure it out he has only one real weakness—that's a base on balls!"

When a pitcher faces a hitter of that type, there's only one thing to do. Give him the best you've got, and don't make them too good. If you can make him hit at a bad ball the chances are he won't hit it squarely. And if he refuses to hit and gets a base on balls it's well to remember Whitey Witt's old wise crack and laugh it off.

Whitey walked over to an opposing pitcher one day after I had walked four times in a row:

"That's the way to pitch," he agreed. "Better four balls for one base than one ball for four bases anytime!"

The smart pitcher is always trying to make the hitter swing at a bad ball. Fellows like Shocker and Pennock and Alex can play those corners to the width of a gnat's eyebrow. In all the innings Alex pitched against the Yankees in the world series I don't believe he threw two balls "down the middle." And when he did the batter was so surprised that he couldn't swing.

And don't think that those corner pitchers don't get on a hitter's nerves after a while. They do. I guess I've looked over as many bad ones as any man in the business in my day and I know. There's nothing more annoying in the world than to step up there at the plate and watch a pitch come floating up big as a balloon but too close or too far out to hit. You can see that it's going to cut the corner, but you know that if you swing the chances are 75 out of 100 that you'll foul it off, or pop it up or roll one to the infield. And if you let it go you know durn well it will be called a strike. After watching pitching of that sort through seven or eight innings you reach the state where you'll swing at anything —which, of course, is just what the pitcher wants you to do.

One of the hardest things for the inexperienced pitcher to learn is when to take things easy and when to bear down. The greatest success of such pitchers as Matty and Three Finger Brown was their ability to judge pace—to take things easy when they had a chance, and then have plenty left to bear down when they had to.

You know one strike out with the bases full and two down is just as valuable as three strikeouts in a row with nobody on and a lot easier. Fans and pitchers new to the game are apt to judge pitching effectiveness by the number of strikeouts and the scarcity of hits in the box score. But the smart pitcher doesn't pay any attention to these things. He takes the slant that it's runs which win ball games and his idea to keep the hits from coming in the pinches. In my experience I've seen pitchers touched for ten or twelve hits and still pitch shut-outs. And I saw little Emil Levsen of Cleveland hold the Yankees to two hits, and lose his game 2 to 0. Of course the fans think the twelve hit pitcher is lucky, while they moan about Levsen's bad luck.

But the facts of the matter are that one pitcher had something when he needed it, and the other fellow failed after some great pitching, simply because he didn't have the strength left to pull out of a pinch. And after you see things like that happen a dozen times a season you come to the conclusion that good pitching is pitching that prevents runs, regardless of base hits.

Another common fault with young pitchers is that they overwork a certain delivery. Perhaps they have a curve ball that's particularly good, or a fast one. The tendency is to keep using that pitch all the time. And take it from me, if you keep using the same thing long enough the hitters will get wise, no matter how deceptive the delivery may be.

Waite Hoyt has a theory that he advances in all the Yankee confabs. "Let 'em see that good one once in a while just so they will know you have it, then put it back in the case until you need it" is Waite's idea.

Hoyt, as I said before is a fast ball pitcher. Yet I've seen him go through a whole game and pitch only eight or ten fast ones in the entire nine innings.

He simply uses that fast one for bait. He shows it to the hitter now and then to let him know that the fast one is still there, then he goes ahead with his curve and half-speed stuff. The hitter gets set for a fast one that never comes, and pops out on half-speeders that catch him off balance. Of course, Waite, has to use the fast one every now and then

53

to keep them guessing, but it's the other stuff that really does the business.

After all, successful pitching is pretty much a matter of keeping the hitter off balance. As long as the man at the plate can't get set, he'll never tear the cover off a ball or break any fences in the outfield. That's the reason a slow ball is so effective. There's nothing about a slow ball to fool any one. Most of them don't curve, and a lot of them don't even wobble. But they do throw a hitter off stride.

When Joe Bush was in form, he was one of the great change of pace pitchers. Joe threw with four distinct speeds. He had a fast one, a halfspeeder, and a couple of varieties of slow pitches. And all thrown with the same motion.

When you'd get set for his fast one he'd cross you up with a slow one; or if you were looking for the slow one the chances are the half-speeder or fast ball would be on you before you could get your bat around. I've seen a lot of curves and a lot of fast ones; I've looked over a lot of trick deliveries of one sort and another and I've hit against pitchers who were supposed to have a lot of stuff.

But after all those years I've about decided that control and a change of pace are the biggest assets

54

a pitcher can have, and curve balls be durned! And I do know this. A curve ball may bother an ordinary hitter, but if a man is a really good hitter it's the old change of pace that causes him more trouble than all the freak deliveries in the world.

The whole secret of a successful change of pace is motion. Good pitchers throw their fast ones and their slow ones with absolutely the same motion. They have to—for hitters and coaches are constantly on the lookout for some little move that will betray the pitch before it comes.

Of all the pitchers in the leagues I don't know one who has a smoother, easier motion than Sam Jones, now with the Washington Senators.

Sam is what we used to call "a motion picture pitcher." His delivery is smooth, easy and graceful and he doesn't vary a bit in anything he throws.

Old Jack Quinn of the Athletics is another man who has a delivery that's a pippin. Jack isn't so easy to watch as Sam. He pitches with more jerk and more effort. But as a bluffer he is in a class by himself.

Jack is one of the few remaining spit-ball pitchers. And he bluffs that spitter on every pitch. Yet he doesn't actually throw it once in six times. Simply goes through the motions and then crosses up the hitter with something entirely different.

But to consider the whole thing briefly. After you've learned control you've taken the first step toward pitching.

Now all you've got to do is develop a curve ball, a fast one, and a change of pace.

Learn to mix them up to keep the hitter off balance.

Perfect a motion that's smooth and easy and deceptive.

Study batters, until you know their hitting style, their little peculiarities and their weakness and strength.

Then, after all that, you're ready to start in on the business of pitching.

CHAPTER V

WHEN I hear the boys talking about pitching
motions I always think of Paul Zahniser, who used
to pitch for Washington and the Red Sox. All
the time Paul was in the big leagues he was a
"cousin" of mine.) (That's what we call pitchers
who are easy to hit. Every time he pitched against
us I knew I would get two or three hits—and so
did he.

But he never knew why. Now that he's back in
the minor leagues again I can tell the secret. I
got hits off Paul because I always knew just what
he was going to pitch. Zahniser had a Walter
Johnson motion. That is he lifted his arms above
his head before he delivered the ball. And after I
faced him once or twice I noticed that on his fast

57

ball he raised his hands far above his head. When he was pitching his curve ball his hands went only as high as his eyes.

Naturally I knew what was coming before he ever threw—and I was all set.

Most pitchers have some little habit in pitching that gives them away. And sometimes it takes a long time before they discover what it is, and correct it. A lot of them never do. Take Herb Pennock's overhand curve ball for instance. Opposing hitters can always tell from Herb's motion just when that overhand curve is coming. Fortunately for Herb that particular curve is such a good one that they can't hit it even when he "telegraphs" it.

I had a habit of my own like that in my pitching days. And I never knew it until I had stopped pitching and had started playing the outfield. Then some of the boys tipped me off.

It all happened one day when we were riding along through Indiana on a Western trip. The boys had been playing cards all morning and along about noon interest in the game began to lag and they started talking baseball. Sherry Smith had beat us the day before, and there's a baby who has a real pitch-

ing motion. Naturally the boys talked about Sherry
and in the course of the conversation I started in
to kid some of our pitchers.

"Why don't you guys get a motion like Sherry's?"
I asked Pennock, "then you'd be real pitchers.
There's one fellow who doesn't telegraph everything
he throws."

Wallie Pipp laughed.

"Listen Big Boy." he said, "let me tell you something. You try to kid these other fellows and you
did more telegraphing in your pitching days than any
of them. That curve ball of yours was a breeze!"

And then Wallie proceeded to tell me that whenever I pitched a curve ball I stuck my tongue out
of the corner of my mouth—a dead give away. And
everybody in the league knew it except me! Imagine
that—a pitcher for four or five seasons, and still telegraphing a curve ball everytime I threw one. It
just goes to show that a pitcher can never be sure
of himself.

And I know Wallie told me the truth that day—
for since I've stopped pitching I've had a dozen different players tell me the same thing. And one day
just for fun I tried it out. I did a little pitching before the game and sure enough, every time I went to

pitch a curve ball, that tongue came sticking out! Naturally no one tipped me off until after my pitching days were over.

Another place where a pitcher needs a good motion is in holding a runner on first base. And there again, is a thing that comes only from practice. Some fellows never get it. I've seen Carl Mays work for a half hour at a time practicing throws to first base, and trying to perfect a throw that started the same as his regular pitching motion. Ed Walsh was a wonder at picking men off. And all left handed pitchers can develop a move pretty easily. That's because as they stand on the rubber they face naturally toward first and can get the ball over with a flip.

The best man I ever saw at picking a man off first base was Sherrod Smith, the old left hander with Brooklyn and Cleveland. There was one chap it wasn't safe to take a five foot lead on. He'd pick you off almost before you knew what happened.

Which reminds me of Hinkey Haines and a thing that happened to him. When Hinkey came to the Yankees from Penn State College he had a reputation for speed on the bases. And he deserved it too. He was as fast as any man in the league. So one day in Cleveland when Sherry was working against us and the game was tight, Hinkey was sent in to run for Schang.

Hinkey trotted down to first base. Charley O'Leary was coaching and before play started Charley walked over and warned Hinkey:

"Now watch that guy," he said, "He's tough. He'll pick you off if you take any lead. Don't go more than three feet off the bag."

Hinkey nodded that he understood and Charley walked back to the coach's box. It's not more than two steps from the bag, but before Charley reached there he heard a yell. Between the time he had finished warning Haines and had walked back to the coacher's box, Sherry had nipped Haines. And caught him flat footed too. That play cost us a ball game—but we all had a laugh on the bench just the same. For there wasn't a man on the club who at some time or another hadn't been a victim of the same play.

What a motion old Sherry has. There isn't another pitcher in the league who can even come close to it.

After a man has been pitching for a time he

just naturally picks up certain tricks of the trade—little things that have nothing to do with the physical side of pitching but have a lot to do with making a man a finished performer.

For instance, suppose your club is one run ahead or tied toward the end of the game. The first man up singles. The next fellow comes to the plate and you know he is going to sacrifice. What do you do?

It's a question that has many an amateur pitcher guessing—but the old-timer doesn't even hesitate. No matter who the hitter is, or what type hitter he may be, the wise pitcher pitches high and fast. And here's why.

When a man is bunting he uses a stiff arm motion, and pushes the ball. With a motion of this sort it's hard for him to reach a ball shoulder high effectively, and still keep control of bat and ball. You can prove that in a minute. Pick up a bat, with hands well separated as if to bunt, and then try and hit an imaginary ball that's on line with your shoulder and just over the inside corner of the plate. See how awkward you feel and how hard it is to reach the given spot effectively.

With a pitch of that sort the hitter seven times out

of ten will foul off the pitch, or will pop up a little fly that can be gathered in by the pitcher or catcher. Better still there's a fifty-fifty chance that he will miss the ball entirely. As I said before that's a little trick of pitching that becomes a habit with the old timer pitcher. It's one of the little things that a man learns by experience.

There are others too. For instance the pitcher must always work in conjunction with his infield and outfield. A hitter is up—say a left hand hitter who naturally hits to right field. The infield and outfield know this and they naturally shift their position to handle a ball hit in that direction. Once shifted, then it's up to the pitcher to see that he makes the hitter send the ball to the right side of the diamond.

And nine times out of ten the method is identical. They pitch inside to a left hand hitter and outside to a right hand hitter. If they want to make sure the hitter hits to left field, the system is reversed.

Naturally there are exceptions—but these are individual cases. And individual hitters are classified by pitchers after a few turns around the league.

In late years slow ball pitching has come to be particularly effective. That's because there are so many free-swinging hitters, and men of this type are apt to be thrown off balance by slow stuff. But just the same the smart experienced pitcher knows that a certain type of hitters cannot be fooled on slow stuff.

Perhaps I can show best what I mean by an actual illustration. Earl Combs, the Yankees' center fielder is a tough man on a slow ball. The pitchers know it. And here's why.

Earl, though a left handed hitter, hits naturally to left field. Which means that he swings late on the ball. That is, instead of hitting out in front of the plate he hits at the back. Naturally if he has a ball properly timed it will go to left field. Now suppose you throw him a slow one. What happens?

Perhaps he's expecting a fast one and swings for such a pitch. Instead of hitting to left field, the lack of speed on the ball permits his bat to come further through and he hits to right. But the point is that he isn't fooled by the slow stuff. He hits it anyway.

When Earl first came into the league a lot of the boys tried pitching slow balls to him. But they have quit it now. It's too dangerous. Seven times

OPENING DAY IN BOSTON, 1927.   RUTH AT BAT, FREDDY HOFMANN
CATCHING, BILL DINEEN UMPIRING

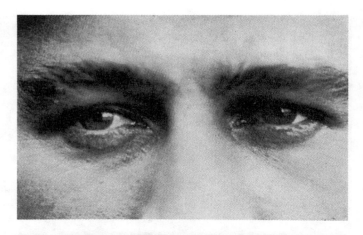

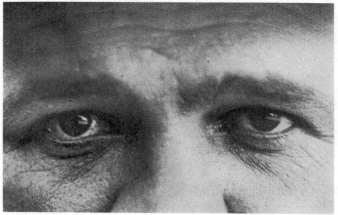

THE EYES HAVE IT! ABOVE—THE KEEN EYES OF LOU GEHRIG. BELOW—THE ORBS THAT PEER AT OPPOSING PITCHERS WHEN THE BABE TAKES HIS STANCE AT THE PLATE

out of ten Earl hits that slow one right on a line through the box and a pitcher has to duck quick or get his head torn off. Back in 1925 when Early was breaking into the league, he sent three pitchers to the hospital in less than a week. He broke Paul Zahniser's ankle, he cracked Joe Bush's knee and he smacked Tom Zachary on the wrist. And each time it was a slow ball he hit.

So far as a hitter of the Combs type is concerned a pitcher can use slow stuff for only one thing. That is to make him hit to right field. But you can't expect to fool him.

With a hitter of my type for instance, it's quite different. I am a free hitter and I "pull" the ball. In other words I swing fast, with a full, free motion and hit the ball out front. Unless I know a slow ball is coming and time my swing accordingly, I miss the slow one simply because my swing is timed to meet the ball out front and I complete my swing at a slow one before the ball ever reaches me.

All of which, again, is just one of the tricks of the trade that a pitcher learns by experience. And there are hundreds of other little stunts that are part of the pitching profession—stunts that can't be taught or explained. They're just little inside pointers that a man must pick up for himself.

But they're the things that mark the difference between a good pitcher and an average one; between a veteran and a rookie. Perhaps you've noticed that our really great pitchers are fellows who have been sticking around for several seasons. A kid may come right up from the sticks and make good as an infielder or an outfielder. A lot of them have done it. Eddie Collins did. So did Frankie Frisch, and George Sisler, and Tony Lazzeri and a half hundred others that you could mention.

But it's very seldom indeed that a pitcher can do it. Even the Mattys and the Browns, the Pennocks and the Vances and the Alexanders had to stick around for several seasons before they finally came through. And it wasn't because they didn't have plenty of stuff, either. It was simply because half of pitching is learning and practicing these little tricks of the business; simply because fifty percent of pitching success is due to pitching knowledge and these things are learned only through long weeks and months of experience.

It's just as Joe Wood used to say when he was in his prime, "The best curve ball in the world isn't worth a plugged nickle until you learn what to do with it—and most fellows never do learn. That's why there aren't very many good pitchers around loose these days."

Another thing that the average kid pitcher overlooks is fielding. And fielding is a mighty important part of a pitcher's business. A pitcher who can't field bunts and slow rolling balls down the base line won't last a season in the big leagues. Allan Sothoron is an example of that. When Allan came into the American League he had as much stuff as any pitcher I ever looked at. And for a few weeks he went great.

Then one day some smart player tried to bunt on him, and Allan kicked the ball all around the infield trying to pick it up. It wasn't three days until every club in the league knew about his weakness, and they proceeded to bunt him right back to the minors. He couldn't field—and three times out of five when a hitter laid one down that Allan had to handle he would either kick the ball around until the runner reached first base, or else in his hurry he'd throw to the stands.

But I'll say this for Sothoron. He knew his weakness as well as anyone. He went back to the minors and the night he left he came around to say good-bye to his buddies.

"Listen you eggs," Allan said, "I'll be back here in a year or two. And when I do I'll be able to field a ball."

He made good too. Once he went back to the minors he started to work on fielding. He would get out and handle bunts for hours at a time, and he even changed his whole pitching motion. And a couple of years ago he came back again. His first time out the gang tried the old bunt stuff and Allan handled seven straight bunts without a bobble. After then the fellows knew that their little trick was all up. Allan Sothoron had got wise. He had learned to field.

The best fielding pitcher I ever saw, I think was George Foster of the old Red Sox. George was sure death on any ball hit to his territory. In three seasons I don't believe I saw him make a single error. He could grab them along the third base line, and he could go over and dig them out at first. More important than that he had a quick underhand throw like an infielder. Urban Shocker is one of the best fielding pitchers of the present day. Eddie Rommell of the Athletics is a fine fielder to. Eddie's fielding ability comes natural. He loves to play ball and when he's not pitching he likes to get out and work around the infield. He does a good job of it too.

Pitchers who are bad fielders usually can correct their fault by a shift in pitching style. Nine times out of ten they are bad fielders simply because they are off balance when they finish the pitch, and they can't shift to go after a ball. The important thing to remember is that the body must follow the throw when pitching. Otherwise the pitcher isn't able to move out of the way of the ball when it's hit back at him. Now and then of course, a ball is hit back so fast that the pitcher hasn't time to move. But nine times out of ten it's the pitcher's own fault if he is hit by a batted ball. He simply isn't shifting his feet right.

If you watch a pitcher like Herb Pennock you'll see that at the finish of his pitch he is balanced forward on his toes, with his weight evenly distributed on both feet. The same motion of his arm that sends the pitch winging across the plate, pulls his body into fielding position without effort. The minute the ball leaves his fingers he is set to field anything that comes his way.

69

And the result is that when Herb is pitching we have nine fielders out there to stop a batting attack. No one else has to do Pennock's work. He does it himself. That's another reason why he's a great pitcher.

CHAPTER VI

WHEN amateurs get together to talk about pitching
there's always a lot of conversation about curve
balls. Most of it is bunk.

In the old days when pitchers were allowed to use
resin, to rough the ball and to pitch dirty, black
battered balls the curve meant something. For in
those days the smart pitcher, taking advantage of
all conditions, could produce some fearful and wonderful "hops" on every pitch.

Given the opportunity, modern pitchers could do
the same thing. Give a fellow like Hoyt or Lyons
or Alexander a ball that has been roughed a little.
They'll show you plenty. And it's easy enough to
understand.

Air friction on the surface of the revolving ball

71

is the cause of a curve. And it doesn't take any master mind to know that a rough surface creates more friction than a smooth hard surface.

When I broke into the big leagues most pitchers were cheating a little. I don't say that as a knock at the pitchers. Perhaps it would be better to say that they took advantage of every opportunity— and there were plenty of opportunities. One of the pet stunts in those days was to load the seams of a ball with dirt to give it added weight on one side. Another popular stunt used to be to work the seams either with finger nails or with some foreign substance like resin or wax. That would tend to raise the seams of the ball a little, thereby giving a better grip at that particular spot.

But the biggest advantage the pitcher had was the fact that umpires permitted them to pitch dirty, battered balls. After a ball has been battered into the dirt a few times, or better still, has been fouled off against a concrete stand, there will be rough spots on the surface. And these rough spots are a pitcher's magic. They not only give him a purchase at the start of his pitch, but they offer resistance to the wind as the ball travels to the plate as well.

THE FAST BALL

After all, the theory of curve ball pitching is simply to apply added friction to the ball on the side to which you want it to curve. On a curve that breaks down, the friction is applied from underneath at the time the ball leaves the pitcher's hand. An outcurve finds the friction (the wrist snap) applied on the outside, a fast ball on the inside, etc.

A pitcher ought to be able to throw a ball that would break up to the batter. A fast ball delivered straight overhand with an upward rotation, would do that. There's one curve though that doesn't work out, simply because the law of gravity overcomes the friction. The result is that a ball delivered overhand with friction from the top comes as near being a straight ball as any a man can throw. As a matter of fact, there is no such thing as an absolutely straight ball. Every ball that is thrown veers a little bit off its course, either from friction or from the force of gravity.

Now and then a pitcher will come along who has enough speed and enough of a grip to give a fast ball an "upward" hop. Waite Hoyt's fast one is that kind. And that's why Waite's fast ball is particularly effective. But it isn't an upward curve.

Just a slight rise at the end that ball players call a "Hop."

Ever since baseball became a popular game the newspaper boys have written stories about freak curves developed by this or that pitcher. You still hear about Matty's "fadeaway," about Joe Bush's "fork ball," about the "screw ball" and the "knuckle" ball and a dozen other freaks of pitching. As a matter of fact there isn't a whole lot of difference between these so-called freaks and the ordinary curves of the ordinary pitcher. Except perhaps that they break a little more quickly or a little wider.

Most of them break down. That's natural enough and easy to understand. For the pitcher who pitches overhand or side-arm, the "drop curve" is the natural curve. For in pitching that one he gets assistance from nature. He has the law of gravity on his side to start with. Naturally friction aided by gravity will produce a bigger, wider curve than friction that is working against the law of gravity.

Most of the "freak" deliveries have been developed because of some hunch on the part of the pitcher. For instance, in my pitching days, the balls we used had printed on them the trade mark

and the name of the league president. It was my hunch that this ink on the side of the ball gave just an added atom of weight to the printed side. Consequently in pitching a curve ball I was careful to hold the inked side of the ball on the side that I wanted the curve to break. A foolish notion, perhaps, but one that I always followed.

In the course of a season I get a couple of hundred letters from kids, I guess, asking me to explain the difference between the various trick curves. That's a tough assignment—for, as a matter of fact, they're all of them pretty much alike.

Take Matty's "fadeaway," Bush's "fork ball," the screw ball, the spitter and Wilcy Moore's famous "sinker." They all break down. They all look much alike as they come zipping up to the plate, and about the only difference is the speed with which they come up.

The theory of the spitter is simple enough. The ball is wet on one side. Naturally that makes a slippery spot which reduces friction and gives added speed to the opposite side where friction is applied. All spit balls break down, but by turning the wet spot one way or the other the pitcher can make the ball break in or out as he desires.

A curve ball from a right hand pitcher, breaks out to a right hand batter usually. Matty's fade-away was a pitch which broke in and down to a right hand hitter. In other words it had the same break as a spit ball, but was a "dry" pitch.

The chief difference between the so-called "screw ball" and the spitter, as I see it is that the screw ball can be thrown only overhand, while the spitter can be thrown overhand or sidearm. Neither pitch can be used by an underhand pitcher. The side-arm spitter is by far the more difficult to handle. Allan Russel, the old time Yankee pitcher who was later with the Washington Senators, was the most successful side-arm spit ball pitcher I ever knew. Allan could break that spitter where he wanted it and since he threw it with the same sweeping side-arm motion with which he delivered his fast ball, it was doubly hard to gauge.

Most of the pitchers in the league today have a screw ball of some sort or another. George Pipgras, the youngster who made good with the Yankees last year, has as good a one as any—though George's knuckle ball is even more effective than his screw ball.

The screw ball like most other pitches, was developed by necessity. After Chesbro and Ed Walsh made the spit ball famous, all the pitchers in the sticks began working to duplicate it. Spit ball pitching was the rage for several seasons. But there were lots of complaints. Catchers complained because they said most pitchers couldn't control their spitter and it was therefore a hard ball to catch. And the infielders kicked because a sloppy wet ball was hard to handle and frequently caused wild throws.

Heine Mueller, one-time Giant and Cardinal outfielder can testify to that I guess. A spit ball cost Heine his job with the Giants and sent him back to the minors. It happened last summer when Heine was playing the outfield in a game which Burleigh Grimes was pitching. Grimes is an old-fashioned spit ball pitcher, and he wets the ball plenty. The hitter got hold of one of Burleigh's spitters and sent it on a line to Heine's sector in center field.

Heinie had been warned about that sloppy ball and he wasn't taking any chance. He grabbed the ball and deliberately wiped it dry on his shirt while a runner scored from third base. And now Heine is back down in the minors, still trying to figure out what to do with that sloppy ball when he gets hold of it.

Anyhow, the kicking against the "spitter" became so loud and strong that the commission finally ruled it out. They decided that spit-ball pitchers already in the league would be permitted to go ahead and use it but that new fellows coming in would have it barred. Naturally the newcomer began looking around for something to take its place and as a result the screw ball was developed. I don't know who was the first to use it. A lot of pitchers claim the credit—but regardless of who happened to be the father, most of the boys have taken it for their own now.

The spit ball, of course, is being used less and less. There are not more than a half dozen spit ball pitchers left in the two leagues. Urban Faber, Urban Shocker, and Jack Quinn still use it in our league. Burleigh Grimes is the leading exponent of the "spitter" remaining in the National League. And these fellows are coming along to the end of their string. Another three or four seasons and there probably won't be a spit ball pitcher left in the majors.

The knuckle ball is another so called "trick" delivery that sounds a lot more dangerous than it really is. The knuckle ball is a slow ball, that comes floating up to the plate without rotating. And lacking that rotation to keep it on a line, it wobbies from side to side. Not far of course, but just enough to throw the hitter off his stride. It isn't the sort of ball that will fool a hitter enough to strike him out—but it's a devilish, tantalizing sort of pitch that you're apt to pop up into the air, or drive into the ground for an easy infield out.

Eddie Rommel was the first man I know to develop a knuckle ball to the point where he really used it as his "ace." Eddie used to toss "knucklers" until he had the hitters blue in the face and he soon got a reputation as the king of the knuckle ball pitchers. But like the rest of the legitimate pitches, it was soon grabbed by the other pitchers and knuckle balls are common things around the league today. And good as Eddie is, I think George Pipgras of the Yankees has the best knuckle ball in the business.

George's knuckler is particularly good too because he has something that Eddie never had. George has a good fast one to mix up with it—and after all, the real success of any pitching depends upon the pitcher's ability to mix up something else with it. The thing that fools a hitter is not the knuckle ball or the screw ball in itself so much as it is having it come floating up there when he expects a fast one or a curve.

At times like that it's really tough!

Of course, when all is said and done, both the knuckle ball and the screw ball are forms of slow ball pitches. Take Herb Pennock for instance. Herb has developed a screw ball in the last few years and he uses it entirely as a change of pace pitch.

It has only been in the last ten or twelve years that the slow ball has come into real prominence. Pitchers threw them before that. Matty had a good one and so did a lot of the old time pitchers. But in those days when hitters were of the choke type and free swingers were uncommon, the slow stuff didn't go over so big. Anyhow, in those days, all the trick stuff was permitted and the slow ball wasn't so badly needed.

But in this day and age a slow ball—"change of pace" the boys call it—is a mighty big factor with most great pitchers. I don't know who was the first pitcher to develop a slow ball. They were

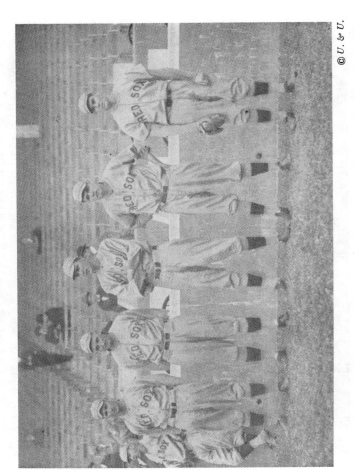

A REMINDER OF PITCHING DAYS. HERE'S THE CHAMPIONSHIP BOSTON RED SOX PITCHING STAFF OF 1915 AND 1916. READING FROM LEFT TO RIGHT: GEORGE FOSTER, CARL MAYS, ERNIE SHORE, BABE RUTH AND HUB LEONARD

GRIPPING THE BALL FOR A CURVE.   RUTH DOUBLES HIS THUMB UNDER.   MANY
PITCHERS USE A GRIP WITH THUMB EXTENDED

throwing them when I came into the league and long before that, I guess. But the best slow ball I've ever looked at was the one thrown by Ray Collins, a big, burly left hander who used to pitch for the Red Sox. Ray threw his slow one with the same identical motion that he threw his fast one and it would come floating up there to the plate without so much as a single revolution. No kidding, a fellow could almost count the stitches on the ball as it came up. And control! Say that Collins had better control of his slow one than most fellows have of their fast ones. He could put that ball right where he wanted it always. I saw him strike Ty Cobb out three times in one game with it, and when a pitcher fans Ty on a slow ball he has to be good. Ordinarily Ty will knock a slow ball right down some infielder's throat.

Collins had a funny way of throwing one too. He would hold the ball with his thumb and little finger, leaving the three middle fingers sticking straight out in the air and not touching the ball at all. Telling about it makes it sound as though it would be easy to tell just when the slow one was coming, but it wasn't. For Ray wouldn't lift those three middle fingers until the very instant he let the ball go.

Waite Hoyt is the only pitcher that I know of in baseball today who throws his slow stuff the same as Collins did. Most of the boys throw knucklers —that is, they double their fingers under and get a grip on the ball with their knuckles. But Waite uses Collins' old system of gripping the ball with the thumb and little finger and leaving the three middle fingers extended.

Like Collins, too, he conceals his pitch well and unless he wants you to see them, you never get a glimpse of those three fingers until the ball is on the way. Waite goes Collins one better though, sometimes. For frequently when he is pitching he'll let those three fingers show as though he had made a mistake. The batter seeing them, thinks a slow one is coming, and gets set for it. Then, just as he is about to release the pitch Waite tightens up his grip and sends a fast one zipping through, catching the hitter off balance and making him look mighty foolish. I've seen him do it a lot of times. And when he's having a particularly good day, with all his stuff, he's apt to pull the stunt a dozen times in a single ball game. And get away with it too.

Goose Goslin is one of his pet victims for that sort of pitching.

The greatest trouble with a slow ball for the average pitcher is that it is mighty hard to control. It is pitched with practically no grip on the ball, and anytime you try to throw a ball without gripping it you're in for trouble. A lot of pitchers, and good ones too, have had to work on a slow ball for years and years before they finally got what they wanted—and even then they're a little bit afraid to use it in a pinch because they don't always know where it is going.

Of course the whole secret of a slow ball is in the fact that it doesn't spin or rotate. It's that failure to spin which makes it travel slowly and wobble on its way to the plate. And it's that thing, too, which makes it tough to hit. For a ball that doesn't spin will never take the "English" from the bat. Hitting a real slow ball is like hitting at a bean bag, or a sack of mush or something like that.

Pitchers, for the most part, can be classified into three divisions. There are fast ball pitchers. These are the pitchers who depend for the most part on a fast ball to carry them through. Then there are "curve ball pitchers" or pitchers who use curves to get past the rough spots. And finally there are what the boys call "mix-up pitchers." These are fellows who mix up a curve with a fast one. "Change of pace" pitchers I guess you might call them.

From my experience in baseball I would say that there were more fast ball pitchers than any other kind. Walter Johnson, when he was in his prime, was the best example of a fast ball pitcher you could find. Walter didn't fool around with curves and he didn't go in for slow stuff. He simply zipped them past so fast that a batter couldn't get his bat around. "Lefty Grove of the Athletics and Rube Walburg and Dazzy Vance are fine examples of fast ball pitchers. So is Charley Root of the Cubs, who made such a great record as an "iron man" last season. Of course these fellows have curve balls too. And good ones. Grove and Walburg both have curve balls that break fast and wide, and they have the added advantage of getting almost as much speed on their curve balls as they do on their fast ones. But just the same they look on their fast ball as their best bet—and always come through with it when they're in a hole.

A lot of experts maintain that a "fast ball pitcher"

will last longer than a curve ball pitcher. They point out that throwing a fast ball isn't as much strain on the arm as a curve. Which is probably true. Still a lot of fellows who were fast ball pitchers originally, have developed into curve ball pitchers once the hop on their fast one began to leave them. Walter Johnson is a fine illustration of that. In the last few years Walter has been depending on curve balls and a change of pace more and more— and its only occasionally that he sends that old "speeder" zipping through there the way he used to.

Herb Pennock is an example of a good curve ball pitcher. Herb has plenty of other stuff, too, but his curve ball is his one big bet. It's the ace up his sleeve. Jess Haines of the Cardinals is another chap who depends upon his curve ball to get him out of trouble. So does Johnny Morrison who used to be an ace with the Pirates.

The mere fact that a chap has a good curve ball, however, doesn't make him a great pitcher. The best curve ball I ever saw was thrown by a fellow who couldn't even make the big league grade, and perhaps never will. That was Walter Beall, who came up to the Yankees a few years ago, but is back in the minors again now. Beall could make a baseball

85

sit up and sing bass, no kidding. His curve broke down, and I'll swear he could break it three or four inches. But he never knew whether it was going over the plate or down the left field foul line—and a curve ball isn't worth a nickle unless the pitcher has control. Maybe some day Walter Beall will get control. When he does, look out for him. He'll be a wizard.

Bob Shawkey is another one who was almost strictly a curve ball pitcher. Bob had that curve of his fooling batters for a good many years before old Dad Time finally got him. Maybe throwing curves is hard on the arm, but it never seemed to bother Bob much. His career was a pretty long and active one, before he finally came to the end of the trail.

The "mix-up pitchers" include such players as Ted Lyons of the White Sox, George Uhle of the Cleveland Indians, Waite Hoyt of the Yankees and Grover Alexander of the Cardinals. These are fellows who mix up fast ones with slow ones. "Change of pace pitchers" I guess would be another name for them. Hoyt and Lyons can throw curves of course. If they couldn't they wouldn't be in the league. But they don't use them often—and usually when they do come up with a curve they keep it outside or inside, where it can't be damaged. For real effectiveness they depend upon a change of pace.

To be a good mix-up pitcher, you've got to have a corking fast ball as well as the slow stuff. Urban Shocker, in the days when he was with the St. Louis Browns, was a pitcher of that sort. And what a tough baby he was too. But of late years Shock has lost his fast one and now he's getting by on his knowledge, plus pitching stuff that includes slow, slower and slowest. Tom Zachary of the Washington Senators falls into about the same class.

But don't think that this classification is absolute. Just remember that the fast ball pitchers all have a curve if they need it and the curve ball boys are apt to cross you up with a fast one anytime.

These I have outlined are the pitches most commonly used by big league pitchers. So far I have made no mention of the trick or freak pitches that come and go with the individual.

In this list come Eddie Cicotte's famous "shine" ball; the emery ball developed and used by Russell Ford, the famous old-time Yankee pitcher, and all the other specialties of certain pitchers. The less the average pitcher knows about these, the better off he is. For they are barred now and an attempt to use them will only get a fellow into trouble.

There's no trick in pitching an emery ball. Once the emery is applied and the ball roughened the greenest pitcher can make the ball do all sorts of queer stunts. And with a little practice he can learn to control and use such curves. But don't do it. It doesn't pay.

As for the others. Well there's Wilcy Moore's "sinker," for instance. That is a fast ball that falls away from the plate. Cy can't tell you himself how he pitches it. It's just natural with him and so far as I know there's no one else in baseball who pitches a ball quite like it. Its effectiveness of course is due to the fact that it sinks away as the hitter swings with the result that he tops the ball and drives it into the ground. If you watch Cy pitch sometime you'll notice that there are always a great many infield putouts in his games. That's the result of the sinker and a mighty puzzling thing it is the first time you face him, too.

Very frequently a pitcher will make a ball "sail" when he pitches it. That usually is due to some unobserved roughness on the cover and is just as apt to be harmful as it is helpful. Now and then however a pitcher will come along with a natural "sailer." He doesn't know himself where he gets it or how. It just happens.

In my pitching days I had little hop on my fast one, despite the fact that I was a fast ball pitcher. But I did have a natural sailer. As I said before I used to think that this was in part due to the added weight given the ball by the trademark stamp, and in pitching I was always careful to turn the ink in the direction I wanted the ball to break. Chances are, though, that this didn't have anything to do with it at all. I'm inclined to think now that it may have been because I gripped the ball very loosely even when pitching my fast one. A lot of fellows will argue that the success of a fast ball depends on the grip and that the fellows with the best fast ones, grip the ball tight. Maybe that's right, but I had a pretty fair fast one, and I used a loose grip always.

I always managed to get a little "sail" on the fast one but there were times when I got more than others. I'll never forget a game I pitched in Detroit one day. My fast one was going great that day and I had the Tigers swinging blind.

Finally Cobb came up. Billy Evans was umpiring and on my first pitch Billy called for the ball and threw it out.

"That one sailed a foot!" he said.

The next pitch was a strike and Cobb called for the ball that time.

"He's doctoring that ball," Ty complained. "That one sailed eighteen inches."

Billy threw that one out.

I pitched a third ball and they both squawked, and that one was tossed out too.

All told I pitched six balls to Ty on that one turn at bat. And after each pitch Billy tossed the ball out of the game.

On the sixth pitch Ty struck out. Boy, maybe you think he wasn't sore.

He walked out past me when the inning was over.

"You're cheating out there you big bum," he said. "No one can make a ball sail like that unless he's doctoring it. But I'll find out about it and when I do I'll run you right out of the league."

As a matter of fact I wasn't cheating. I was just as puzzled as Ty. And to this day I don't know what made those balls sail. They broke so wide that Bill Carrigan who was catching, had to hop all over the plate to get them. And I never had so much "sail" before or since.

It was just one of those things. I don't know why or how I did it. It just happened. Baseball is like that and the longer you play the game the more you realize it.

CHAPTER VII

IN the 1927 world series there were a lot of plays
that stood out. One of the prettiest plays I ever
saw was Joe Dugan's fielding and throw of a slow
bunt down the third base line in that final game.
But by that time most of the fight had been taken
out of the Pirates anyhow, and Joe's contribution
was just one more to a long list of breath-takers.

One of the most important plays of the series so
far as its after effect was concerned, came in the
first game, and Tony Lazzeri was the boy who pulled
it. The details, as I remember them, were about like
this.

George Grantham, a sweet ball player and a
mighty fast man on the bases, was first up to open

the inning. He worked Hoyt for a base on balls and the stage was set for a sharp Pirate attack. Joe Harris, one of the best of the Pirate hitters, followed Grantham at the plate and he signalled Grantham for the hit and run. Just as Hoyt drew back to pitch Grantham leaped for second and Joe Harris smacked the ball squarely on the nose. Lazzeri had leaned toward second with the pitch and was starting as if to cover, but caught himself in time. With perfect timing he scooped up the ball and tagged Grantham out as he tore for second. Then with the same motion he shot the ball to Gehrig and Harris was doubled at first base.

So far as actual play was concerned the play was good and snappy, but not spectacular. But it was a death blow to the Pirates just the same. For when that play was pulled it showed them that we had an infield that could click under pressure, and a second baseman who knew what to do in the face of a hit and run attack. Right off the bat it made the Pirates doubtful about their best attacking method, and when a bit later, Tony pulled the same play they were thoroughly convinced.

The point is that second base is the pivot of all infield play. Give any ball club a second baseman and a short-stop who can work together in perfect harmony with each knowing the other's style and methods and you've solved four-fifths of the infield troubles right there. By that I don't mean that the second baseman and the shortstop must be stars. There are mighty few real stars there, or elsewhere. But there are some mighty sweet ball players—and the minute you get two who can work together you've got a rare combination.

As a matter of fact the best pair I ever saw around second base weren't in the big leagues at all. They were Neil Ball and Clyde Derrick, and they were playing with the Baltimore Orioles when I broke in. Ball had been a star at one time, but when I knew him his career was about closed. Old time fans will remember him. He's one of the few big league players who ever made a triple play unassisted. As for Derrick, I don't think he ever gained any great fame.

Just the same though, playing together, they were a great combination. One seemed to know, always, just what the other would do—and I've seen them field and throw balls without even looking, they were so confident that the other would be there to make the play. Their best stunt was going over back of second base to field balls that looked like sure base hits, and no matter which one went after the ball, the other was right on hand to keep it winging on its way.

Just how important that second base combination is, can be shown by the fact that 99 percent of the teams that win pennants are strong in that department. They may be weak elsewhere: they may have only fair pitching or poor outfielding, or maybe a weakness at first or third or behind the bat—but almost always you find them with a great combination at second and short. From what the old-timers tell me, Joe Tinker and Johnny Evers must have been about as great as any of them. I never saw them working together, but they had to have something to be remembered through all these years.

Of the big league combinations I have seen, there are three or four that stick out in my mind. Barry and Collins of the old Athletics were one pair. Eddie was the master mind of that outfit, and he continued to shine as a second baseman long after Jack Barry was through. Eddie left the Athletics to go with the White Sox, and there he paired up with Risberg and Buck Weaver. There was another great combination.

Probably no other two men on the club had more to do with the Washington victory in 1924 and 1925 than Bucky Harris and Roger Peckinpaugh. Peck, incidentally, is the best shortstop I ever knew, I think. In his prime he could do everything that anyone would ask—and in addition he knew his baseball from front to back. He was smart, and one of the best points he had was an uncanny ability to size up a play.

One of the pet tricks of some smart hitters—fellows like Cobb and Collins and hitters of that type—is to fake a swing to draw the shortstop out of position, and then hit one through him. In all the time I have been in the league I've never seen Peck fooled on that play, and I've seen fellows try it a lot. In fact I've tried it myself, and nearly twisted my neck out of joint trying to snap the ball to left field.

Naturally I don't know so much about the National League. I see those players only in world series games and occasionally during the summer when we have an off day, but I did see enough of the Giants to know that Bancroft and Frisch made a great pair around second. Like Peckinpaugh with Harris, Bancroft was the boy who supplied the quick

ROGERS HORNSBY, ONE OF THE GREATEST BALL PLAYERS OF ALL TIME, SHOWS HOW HE GOES
AFTER A GROUND BALL

OUT! HERBIE PENNOCK ATTEMPTS A STEAL BUT IS OUT AT THE BAG. NOTE HOW BASEMAN HAS
SUCCESSFULLY BLOCKED THE BASE TO PREVENT PENNOCK SLIDING AROUND HIM

© U. & U.

thinking and Frankie came through with the smart mechanical stuff. Some of the plays that pair pulled against us in the 1923 world series were plain and simple murder. I've never asked John McGraw point blank, but I've got a hunch that if you asked him to name the two men on his club most responsible for the Giant pennants in 1922 and 1923, Banny and Frank are the players he would name.

Aside from the mere ability to dig balls out of the dirt, the most important requirement for a good second baseman or shortstop, as I see it, is the ability to throw from any position, and to snap the ball with both speed and control. That's because of the double play. And don't mistake the importance of that two-ply killing. It's the greatest single item in a team's defense.

Up in the big leagues we always sort of take it for granted that a ground ball to the infield will be one out. But it's the fellows who are in there getting two at a time who really take rank as stars. And double plays aren't easy. The place where most infielders fall down on a double play is in pivoting for the throw. That's where Bucky Harris of the Washington Senators is a past master. Bucky makes his pivot, tags his man if necessary, and gets the ball away to first all with the same motion. And on a play of that sort the split part of a second means the difference between a runner being out or safe.

In throwing, the weight, at the time the ball is delivered, is on the left foot. (That is for right hand throwers and all infielders except first basemen are usually right handed.) Naturally in making a double play, if you can touch second with your left foot and throw at the moment your foot touches the bag you can make the play more quickly than if you tag up with your right foot and then have to take a step forward for the throw. Watch Bucky sometime and you'll see that nine times out of ten he tags up with his left foot and goes right on through with his motion. Sometimes of course that is impossible, and then he resorts to a quick, underhand snap throw. But the other is best, and he uses it most of the time.

The shortstop should have an arm that is nearly perfect. His throws are longer than those of the second baseman, and usually must be delivered with more speed because he makes his plays deeper and the batter gets a longer start on balls hit to short. Everett Scott, the old Yankee and Red Sox "iron man" was one of the most accurate throwers I ever saw in the shortfield. Scotty "trolley wired" his throws as the boys say. In other words, he sent them on the same straight line every time, as though the ball was traveling on some invisible wire.

One of the best throwing arms in the league today is possessed by young Reeves, a rookie brought up by the Washington Senators last year. That kid throws like a bullet and right to the mark. He isn't much of a hitter and I'm not sure he's good enough in the field to make the grade, but he certainly can toss that onion. Travis Jackson of the Giants is another great thrower.

The boys tell a story of a play Travis made in Cincinnati the year he broke in. Poor old Jake Daubert was playing with the Reds then and he hit a hot ground ball through the box and just inside second base. Jake took one look and started jogging to first base. That hit had base hit labeled all over it.

But Jackson went across fast, grabbed the ball out of the dirt, with one hand, then straightened up and sent the ball whizzing like a bullet to Kelly. Daubert was out by half a stride and went back to the bench cussing to himself.

"What a play," some of the boys on the bench remarked. "There isn't another shortstop in the league could have made it!"

"Yeh and nobody but that young fool out there would even have tried it," was Jake's reply.

One of the toughest plays that either a shortstop or second baseman is called upon to make, is to go back into the short outfield for high pop flies. Taking a ball in front of you is one thing, but running back to take a fly ball over your shoulder is something else again. Some of the boys never do get the knack of it.

Rogers Hornsby is one of the fellows who find this a tough job. Rog is a great second baseman— one of the greatest of all time—but he can't go after pop flies as he should. He has tried and tried, and down South they tell me he practices by the hour, but somehow he can't seem to get the hang of it.

Frankie Frisch and Tony Lazzeri, on the other hand, are wizards at this particular stunt. I've seen Frisch go way over to the right field foul line and come up with the ball. And one of the greatest plays I've ever seen in my whole career was pulled by Frankie Frisch in the 1923 world series when he went into center field back of second base, leaped in the air and caught Ward's pop fly over his shoulder with one hand, and then whirled and threw to the plate in time to catch Dugan scoring from third.

Of all the difficult plays I've ever seen, that one still stands out in my mind as the greatest.

People have asked me why it is the second baseman and shortstop go into right or left for pop flies instead of the first or third baseman. The answer is easy. They're in better position to see the ball and the play. If a first baseman goes into right field for a pop fly he has to turn his back. The same with a third baseman on a pop fly to left. But the second baseman or shortstop can run at an angle and still keep their eye on the ball throughout its flight. It's the old, old story that a man can make more speed running forward than he can backward, and you've got a better chance of catching a ball that you can see in flight than you have of taking one blind, over your shoulder. This again is a play that can be perfected only by constant practice. Mark Koenig is a fine example of that. Mark is one of those nervous, high strung fellows who will undergo real agony while standing under a pop fly waiting for it to come down. The first year Mark was with the Yankees he kicked pop flies all around the place. He was so bad that once he was hit in the face by a falling ball, and two or three times he got hit on the chest and arms.

But he kept trying—and last season he had so improved himself that he went through the entire season without dropping a single pop fly that he was able to get his hands on.

The first requirement of good play at second and short is complete understanding and cooperation. You've got to have a set of signals—we always call them "signs" in baseball—that are quickly and easily understood so there will be no mistaking as to who is to cover the bag or take the throw. Sometimes of course signs are not necessary. With a man on first base and a natural right field hitter up, the second baseman naturally plays over and the shortstop covers up. On a left field hitter the play is exactly opposite. Those are what we call "naturals."

But there are a lot of other situations that arise when it is absolutely necessary for the shortstop and second baseman to have signs. And it's a lot better if the pitcher, catcher, and other infielders know what is happening too. Then there's very little chance for a mix-up.

Another confusing play for the beginner at second base is the handling of a drag bunt or slow roller between first and the pitcher's box. There's no rule for such a play. It's just a matter of practice and understanding between the first and second baseman. If the ball is within reach of the first baseman, then it's up to the second baseman to cover first and take the throw. Otherwise the first baseman holds his bag and the second baseman fields the ball.

Speaking of drag bunts, that is one of the greatest weaknesses in the Yankees' infield play. Tony Lazzeri and Lou Gehrig have played tiddle-winks on more drag bunts and slow rollers than any pair I ever knew. Lou somehow just can't get the knack of judging balls like that and at times he drives Tony nutty. But he's improving—and in another season or two he'll have the thing down pat.

But even the ability to do all the things I've outlined above—and do them well—doesn't mean that a man will be a great infielder. There's still that business of "tagging the runner" to look out for and that isn't easy at all. Tagging a man properly is an art. I've seen some great looking kids come up to the big leagues, kids who seemed to have everything. But they didn't stick, because they couldn't "put the ball on the runner."

Eddie Collins is a master in this specialty. Eddie

always manages to get squarely between the runner and the bag, and let the runner slide into the ball. A lot of players are spike shy. That is, they're just a little bit afraid of the spikes as a runner comes sliding into the bag. A spike shy player will never make an infielder. It can't be done.

I never knew John Evers in his prime, but I guess John must have been a master at putting the ball on a runner. One of the best yarns I ever heard Casey Stengel tell was about his experiences when he broke in. His first time up he got a hit and a moment later went sliding into second base past Evers.

Casey was a fresh rookie and always had something to say. He said it this time.

"I thought you were such a whiz around that second bag," Casey said to Evers. "But I was a little too smooth for you, eh? Are you the best they have in this league?"

"Listen, Rookie" Johnny replied, "the next time you come down here you'd better wear a tin helmet. I'm going to slam that ball right down your throat!"

"And," says Casey, "he did it too!"

In the old days base runners used to go into the bag with their spikes high intentionally. Basemen were considered fair game at all times, and if the base runner could cut the legs or hands or arms of the basemen he did it. By the same rule the baseman felt free to tag the runner out with a swing to the jaw or any other tender portion of his body. Basemen, too, in the old days had a little trick of jumping in the air and coming down on the hands and legs of the runner as he slid.

Those days are pretty much past now. Deliberate spiking isn't permitted any more, and when such things occur in these days it's a hundred to one that it was an accident pure and simple. None the less there's always danger so long as men slide—and always will be. And the good baseman is on his guard. The ability to tag fast and get away has saved many a pair of shins. It's part of the art of infield play.

CHAPTER VIII

I CAN remember as a kid that an outfielder's job
was looked upon as a sort of necessary evil. Nobody wanted to be a fielder, and the poorest, slowest,
littlest fellows in the game were the ones who were
chased out to the "gardens."

Ring Lardner or one of the baseball humorists
once wrote a wise crack about that same thing. "They
call it left field," he wrote, "because they fill all the
other places first and then if there's any one left they
send him out there."

Kids have funny ideas. Back in my kid days the
fellow who was lucky enough to own a ball or a
bat naturally became captain of the team. And the
captain always appointed himself pitcher. If we
had some stocky, fat kid in the gang we made him

a shortstop on the hunch that balls hit to short were always fast and hard and it took a stocky kid to field them. Little fellows were always made into second basemen. Maybe that was because John Evers of the Cubs and Miller Huggins of the Cincinnati Reds were in their prime then, and they were small men.

And of course playing the outfield was the crowning insult. Nobody wanted to go out there—and many a kid fight developed over who had to "chase flies" in the outer gardens.

As a matter of fact the outfield is a mighty important post in baseball, and some of the greatest stars the game has known have been outfielders. Men like Harry Hooper, Tris Speaker, Ty Cobb, Eddie Roush, Paul Waner, Goose Goslin, Frank Schulte and fellows of that type have played a big part in the development of baseball.

And outfielders today, have got to have a lot of ability, if they expect to hold their jobs.

They've got to have speed and be able to get underway quickly. More than any other players on the club, they must have the ability to judge the flight of a hard-hit ball and do it instantly. They must be able to throw far and accurately, and above all else they must be able to stand up there at the plate and hit the ball.

Managers of the big league ball clubs today, frequently will carry a second baseman or a short stop on his fielding ability. They're willing to sacrifice a little hitting ability for the sake of smooth infield defense. But an outfielder is expected to be a hitter —and if he can't hit he won't last long.

So far as actual work is concerned the outfielder has one of the easiest jobs on the ball club. Even on a busy day he isn't called upon to handle more than six or eight chances, and there are scores of games during the course of the season when he never handles a single ball. Nor is he called upon to make the quick starts and stops, the snap throws or the hurried plays that are required of an infielder. The strain isn't so great on his arms and his legs. The result is that the playing life of an outfielder is usually longer than that of an infielder.

Baseball history proves the statement. Eddie Collins is the only infielder in either league right now, who has been in the game for fifteen years. There have been several outfielders whose careers covered that long or longer. Ty Cobb, Tris Speaker, Zach Wheat, Max Carey—all of them went well

108

past the fifteen year mark. So did Willie Keeler, Jimmy Sheckard, King Kelly and a lot of the old-timers.

Outfield play has changed a lot in the last few years. Fifteen years ago, before the rabbit ball came into existence, and in the era when hitters choked their hits and tried for direction more than distance, the outfielders ranged close in. They took more chances on a ball going over their heads, than they do now. And they were called upon to do a lot more throwing. A strong throwing arm was absolutely necessary to an outfielder ten years ago —and many a run was cut down at the plate by a good throw.

Now, however, since the rabbit ball has come into being and hitters are aiming at the fences, the outfielders play far out and the throwing end of the game is not as important as it once was. The distances are so great that a throw home from most outfield positions is almost impossible. And center fielders in particular have little or no chance to nail their man on a long fly. And by the way, that explains why managers arrange their outfielders to put the weak thrower in center field, if possible.

Don't get me wrong. A great throwing arm is

still a mighty helpful thing to an outfielder. But not so necessary as it used to be. A fellow with a weak arm can hold a job these days. Fifteen years ago he would have been turned loose.

There are some mighty sweet throwing arms among the big league outfielders today. Bob Meusel of the Yankees, has one of the greatest arms in the business. I've seen Bob make a running catch in left field and then throw to first base for a double play. That's real throwing. And with Bob playing left field, there are mighty few runners will score from third base on a short fly to left. He's caught so many of them that they're all scared now. They don't even try to take a base on him.

Harry Rice, the little outfielder who used to be with the Browns and is now with the Tigers, is another boy who can whip that ball around. So can the Waner brothers of the Pittsburg Pirates.

This subject brings up a rather interesting point. A lot of folks figure that my pitching experience has helped me in making throws from the outfield. Personally I don't think so. The pitching throw is entirely different from the outfield throw. The pitcher uses a snap motion to give the ball a "hop." The outfield throw is long and smooth and easy.

OUTFIELD THROWING

It has more of the full arm and less of the wrist than a pitching throw.

One of the fellows who has managed to get by in big league baseball despite a weak arm is Eddie Brown of the Boston Braves. I'm told Eddie can't throw a lick—and opposing teams all know it. But playing in center field he finds little occasion for real throwing, and he always has the aid of his infield in making a relay. And what he lacks in throwing power he more than makes up in his ability to "go get 'em" and to slam that ball on the nose.

John McGraw tried an interesting experiment a few years ago when he had George Kelly at first base and some indifferent throwers in the outfield. On fly balls that required a play at the plate John would send Kelly scampering into the outfield to relay the throw. I've seen him go chasing all the way from first base to deep short to help Irish Meusel get the ball back, and it wasn't at all unusual to see him stepping out to short center to grab a throw from Jimmy O'Connell.

Kelly had and still has one of the greatest throwing arms in the business. The Yankees know it and how! One of the greatest plays ever pulled in a world series was pulled by this same Kelly in 1923.

Joe Dugan was on third base and I was at bat. I got hold of a fast ball and sent it down the first base line a mile a minute. It looked like a two bagger sure. But somehow Kelly managed to get over to the ball and knocked it down with his gloved hand. That ball rolled about three feet away but he was after it like a flash, and then without even straightening up he shot the ball to Frank Snyder at the plate in time to get Dugan trying to score from third base. Nobody but Kelly could have made that play. That was one instance where a great throwing arm meant a ball game—for that single play beat us out. The boys were whipped the minute it was pulled.

I've seen a lot of great outfielders come and go since I've been in the big leagues. I saw Ty Cobb when he was in his prime—though Ty never was as great a defensive player as he was a hitter. He's one star who was hampered by a rather weak arm, and he had a weakness on ground balls too.

Tris Speaker was right at the top of his game when I broke in too—and Tris at his best came mighty near being the daddy of all fly-chasers. But I think there's one man in my experience who was even better than Cobb and Speaker. He comes about

Wide World Photos

GENERAL VIEW OF THE PLAYING FIELD AND CROWD AT THE THIRD GAME OF THE 1927 WORLD
SERIES.   RUTH AT BAT, LEE MEADOWS PITCHING

Wide World Photos

HERE SHE COMES! THE BABE GOES BACK TO THE FENCE FOR A LONG FLY

as near being the perfect outfielder as any man I ever saw. And that was Harry Hooper, the great Red Sox outfielder who finally ended his career with the Chicago White Sox. Harry Hooper had everything. He could hit, he could field and he could throw. I never saw a man who could go back on a ball as well as Harry. Most outfielders, when a ball is hit over their head, run sideways in an effort to keep their eye on the ball all the time.

But not Harry. He would take one squint, then turn his back and run to the place where the ball was headed. And in all his career I don't believe he misjudged a half dozen balls. Few outfielders can do that. Following a fly ball in flight and catching it is one thing. But turning your back at the crack of the bat and running at top speed, then turning in time to grab the ball out of the air is something else again.

Harry could come in on a ball too, with the best of them. Coming in to take a ball at the shoe strings, of course, was Tris Speaker's best stunt. There was no one quite in his class, but Harry came pretty close. And if Speaker was a little heavier hitter—he certainly was no better than Hooper in a pinch.

Hooper and Speaker were playing together in Boston when I broke in, and with them was Duffy Lewis. What an outfield! Perhaps not the best of all time, but one of the best. Duffy rated right along with the other two. A funny fellow was Duffy Lewis. One of the pleasantest, squarest, friendliest fellows in baseball, he had more friends than any player I ever knew. He had a fad for dress too— and he certainly was the clothes horse of the league. His neckties used to be the envy of everyone on the circuit, and I never saw him when he didn't look as though he had just stepped out of a tailor shop.

There are a lot of well-dressed men in baseball. Waite Hoyt is a regular tailor's model and Clarence Rowland and Billy Evans, the umpires, were the "glass of fashion" and the "mould of form," as the style experts call it. Bill Veeck of the Cubs is another neat dresser, and Bob Meusel always looks like the advertisements of what the well-dressed man will wear. But none of them had anything on Duffy Lewis. He was old Kid Fashion himself.

Speaker, Lewis and Hooper taught me about everything I know about playing the outfield. They were students of the game always, and mighty few tricks of the outfielding trade ever got by them.

PLAYING THE HITTER

I've heard them, sitting around the clubhouse in Boston, go right down the list of American league hitters and tell where each one hit, and why. They weren't content to know that Joe Judge, for instance, was usually a right field hitter. They wanted to know where Joe hit a fast one and a slow one, what he did with a high ball outside or a low one inside, and they always insisted on knowing just what the pitcher was going to do with each ball he pitched.

That's the most important part of an outfielder's business. Too many amateurs figure that all an outfielder has to do is go out there and chase flies. But the real outfielder studies the hitters as closely as does the pitcher. They shift with every man who comes to the plate, moving in and back and to and fro like a lot of policemen looking for a riot.

One of the best men in the business today at judging a hitter is Max Carey, the old Pirate captain, now with the Brooklyn Robins. Max has lost a lot of his speed, and the old throwing arm isn't what it used to be, but he can still judge a ball before it is hit with the best of them. And it keeps him out there playing regularly while a lot of other fellows, faster and better mechanically, are picking up splinters on the bench.

Of course there are a few general rules. A left hand hitter for instance is apt to be a right field hitter, while a right hand hitter is more apt to hit to left or center field. With a fast ball pitcher working, outfielders as a rule, play a little further back than when a slow ball pitcher is working. But these rules are not iron-bound, and the good outfielder never sticks too close to such rules. He views the hitter as an individual and studies his individual style, knowing that two men who hit in much the same fashion may still hit to opposite fields.

One of the best all around outfielders in the business today is Al Simmons of the Athletics. He has a peculiar fielding style. Simmons takes a long loping stride when running, and from the stands it doesn't appear as though he covered much ground. But when you've hit a few out his direction and seen him gallop across after them, you realize your dope is all wrong. Al is squatter and heavier than the average outfielder too.

If you pay particular attention you'll find that most outfielders are of the greyhound type—slim, with long legs, and inclined to "skinnyness." Bob Meusel and Earl Combs of the Yankees are of this type. Ty Cobb used to be, though in recent years he is filling out and putting on weight. Sam Rice of the Washington Senators—a whale of an outfielder in his prime, Kenny Williams of the Boston Red Sox, Eddie Roush of the Giants, Max Carey of the Brooklyn club all are of that general type.

Though of course there are exceptions. For instance I've been playing the outfield for some years, and no one can say I have a boyish form. And then there's Al Simmons, mentioned before, and Hack Wilson of the Cubs and Bob Fothergill of the Tigers. Round, tubby fellows all of them. But they get their speed in spite of their weight, not because of it.

One of the greatest outfielders the game has known in recent years is Johnny Mostil of the White Sox. Johnny is one of the fastest men after a fly ball I ever saw. He made a catch off me in White Sox park a couple of seasons ago that was a heartbreaker. The ball was hit far over his head to the center field wall. He turned his back with the crack of the bat and sped at full tilt to the wall, then turned and took the ball with a leap. Naturally he crashed into the concrete and how he held it is more than I can figure. But he did—for one of the greatest outfield plays I ever saw, and one that robbed me of a home run.

Two other great outfield plays stand out in my mind, of all I have seen. One was made by Bib Falk of the White Sox. He was playing left field at the Stadium and with Joe Bush up as a pinch hitter, Bib played well back and over toward center. Joe hit a line drive over third base and down the foul line. Bib came in fast, made a last dive for the ball and caught it as he was sliding along on his stomach. He took the ball with the gloved hand, not more than two inches off the ground, and then turned a complete flip-flop across the cinder path. His face and both arms were cut with the cinders and when he came to the bench he was covered with blood. But he held the ball.

The other outstanding catch I remember was Sam Rice's play on Earl Smith's long liner in the 1925 world series—a play which won the game for the Senators and came near starting a baseball war.

You probably remember how it all happened. The Pirates were a run behind with two out and two on when Earl hit this one. It had home run labeled all over it and was headed squarely for the temporary bleachers in center field. But Sam came tearing across, made a dive and took the ball just as he tumbled over the low railing and into the crowd. There's still a lot of argument as to whether or not he held the ball. But the umpires said he did and I'm willing to take their word for it. Anyhow it was a great performance.

Hitters, of course, are always trying to cross up outfielders. Now and then they get away with it. One of the best laughs I ever had in my life was at the expense of Charley Jamieson, the Cleveland left fielder, and a good one too. Over in Cleveland the outfield plays me entirely to right. The right fielder moves back to the wall, close to the foul line. The center fielder goes over to the right field wall in right center and the left fielder swings around to deep center. That leaves left field wide open.

This particular day I saw Jamieson way over in center and decided to try and push the ball to left. Uhle was pitching and whether he was attempting to cross me up or simply made a mistake I don't know. Anyhow he pitched inside and I got a perfect drive down the third base line. It looked like a three bagger sure, but the sight of Jamieson tearing across that field on his little short legs as if somebody was chasing him got to me. I was laughing as I left the plate and I was laughing as I turned first base. So were the fans and the rest of the Cleveland club. It was a lot funnier to see than it was to tell about, and I got laughing so hard that instead of reaching third base I only got to second.

I've seen outfielders crossed up a lot in my day, but I never saw one as completely fooled as Jamie was that time—and how he ran, trying to get back into left field and grab that ball!

Which is just about the story of outfielding except this. Catching fly balls, judging them for height, distance and direction is simply a matter of practice. Even the best outfielders after a winter's lay off, look foolish on fly balls when they start to work in the spring. You've got to chase them, and chase them, and then chase them some more. Practice and practice alone will do it!

And if a man isn't willing to practice hard and long he better stick out of the outfield. Otherwise he's apt to get one in the head some day and be carted to the hospital.

CHAPTER IX

THE most important player in the ball game, so far as keeping the team working together and directing defensive play is concerned, is the fellow with the mask and the protector back of the plate.

You don't hear a lot about the catcher. Mostly the cheers are for the other fellows. By the very nature of his job he can't be sensational. Just a hard-working, plugging ball player. But without a good catcher it is mighty tough going, believe me.

Two things in particular make the catcher a man to look out for. In the first place he's the one who directs the pitching, giving signals to the pitcher as what to pitch and when, and where. Of course with an old, experienced pitcher this isn't so important. For the old-timer, having had a chance to study the hitters, knows as much about them as the catcher himself. And frequently the pitcher will "shake off" the catcher's signal. That is, he will change the catcher's signal for one of his own.

But with kid pitchers the catcher is the works. He can make them or break them. Catchers like Johnny Kling of the old Cubs, Roger Bresnahan of the Giants, Muddy Ruel of the Senators and Ray Schalk of the White Sox deserve as much credit as the pitcher himself for a well pitched game. Fellows like that do more than simply catch the balls that are thrown by the pitcher. They pitch right along with him, steadying him when he needs steadying, boosting him up when encouragement is needed, and making his way easy as possible always. That's real catching when a man does that.

Of course there are some ball clubs where the work of the catcher is entirely mechanical. The Giants are an example of that. John McGraw has long held that he would do the thinking for his ball club. He gives the signs and calls for the pitch. His catchers do what they're told, and call for the pitch as McGraw himself signals. Sometimes it works out well and sometimes not so well. But Mac is perfectly frank about it.

DIRECTING THE PLAY

"You do as I tell you, and I'll take the blame for whatever happens," he says. And he does it, too!

In the world series between the Yankees and the Giants Snyder, Gowdy and Smith, who did the Giant catching, used to turn toward the bench for their signal on every pitch. We used to kid them about it a lot—but Mac never let up. Though it did seem to me he gave Gowdy a little more leeway than he did the other two. Now and then Hank would be permitted to do his own thinking. But then Gowdy was an old, experienced man who knew the McGraw system from top to bottom.

Ordinarily though, the catcher is given free rein and is responsible for the signs and the pitches. On our club for instance, Hug now and then in a tight place will give the catcher instructions—but for the most part he lets them play their own game.

The second important job of the catcher outside his mechancal work is to boss the defensive play. A lot of people have never realized it, but if you take a good look at the diamond you'll realize a peculiar thing. That is this. The catcher is the only man on the club so placed that every single play occurs before his eyes. The pitcher has five men working behind his back. The second baseman can't see the outfield. The first baseman can't see right and center field and he has only a partial view of left field and third base. But the catcher, by reason of his position facing the play, sees them all—and is in a position to direct the play of the others.

On an infield fly it is the catcher who calls the man to take the ball; on an attempted steal it is the catcher who is in position to warn the others. He has to have his eyes open all the time, and a team that has poor catching is handicapped from the start.

So far as a pitcher is concerned, good catching means everything to him and poor catching means his ruination. That's true even of veteran pitchers. No matter how much natural stuff a pitcher may have he can't pitch well unless he has absolute confidence in his catcher. And certain pitchers and catchers work together so long that the pitcher is lost pitching to any other man. Mathewson and Myers were such a team. Matty always pitched to Myers and despite the fact that Bresnahan was a great catcher, he and Matty never were able to team up successfully. Roger on the other hand could handle Bugs Raymond like a whiz, while Myers was lost with Bugs' pitching.

Baseball history is full of famous batteries. Brown

and Kling of the old Cubs were a great pair. So were Walsh and Sullivan of the famous old Hitless Wonder White Sox. Lou Criger and Cy Young worked together perfectly for a good many years, and Johnson and Street rode to fame together with Walter's fast one. After Gabby left the big leagues Eddie Ainsmith took up the burden and for a long time it was Johnson and Ainsmith who figured in the announcement of the batteries.

I almost called it the umpire's announcement. It's a funny thing how people accept a false statement as fact, simply because of long repetition. Even the newspaper boys tell in their yarns about the umpire announcing the battery. As a matter of fact the umpire doesn't announce the batteries at all. A long time ago the umpires were the announcers, but in the last fifteen years the various clubs have employed professional announcers to do this work. Anyway, the fans still talk about the umpires announcing the batteries and I suppose they always will.

Once they get an idea they cling to it. For instance when Walter Johnson broke into the big leagues he was a fast ball pitcher and even to this day Walter's fast one is the subject of many a baseball powwow. As matter of fact, Walter's fast one has been slowed up for a long time and in its place he has developed a curve ball that's a peach. But they still talk about that fast one and the curve is seldom mentioned, except by the players themselves. Believe me, we know the difference.

Frank Snyder, the old Giant and Cardinal catcher, now manager of the Houston club, was the victim of just such publicity. When Frank broke into the league he was called a "sucker" on pop fouls. Couldn't seem to catch them to save his soul. Naturally the word went out that he was weak on fouls. Snyder overcame that weakness long, long ago. Right now there isn't a better man on foul flies in either league than Snyder. But the idea got out, and in the minds of the fans he's still as much a sucker as the day he broke in.

Speaking of foul flies—there's one of the toughest things a catcher is called upon to handle. Catching a high fly directly over your head is never easy, and when you're hampered by a mask and protector in addition, it's twice as tough. In catching a foul fly the catcher must first locate the ball, then he has to discard his mask and start moving. And always, you must remember, he's handicapped by the closeness of the backstop and stands, and the fact that he's within verbal range of the fans and the **rival** bench as well.

Like catching flies in the outfield, catching fouls back of the plate is entirely a matter of practice. But there's this difference. The outfielder, facing the play, can see the ball from the minute it leaves the bat. The catcher doesn't see it at all. He hears it nick the bat and senses that it's somewhere in the air over his head. The pitcher usually yells to him as to its direction and whether or not he can get it. So do the fellows on his own bench. But their voices very likely are drowned out by the fake advice that comes from the rival bench. It's up to him to locate that ball quickly, and if you think that's an easy job, just try it.

I mentioned Frank Snyder and his foul fly weakness before. Frank overcame it wonderfully—and did it by practice. He used to go out to the park after the other fellows had gone and get someone to hit high flies for a half hour at a time. Gradually he developed his sense of direction and then he started to improve. Today he's almost perfect in that department.

The greatest bit of foul fly catching I ever saw happened in Philadelphia last season. Johnny Grabowski made the catch, and wonderful as it was, it came near costing us a ball game. We were engaged in one of those nip and tuck thrillers with the A's. Eddie Collins was on third base and Ty Cobb on first when Al Simmons raised a foul that was headed for the A's dugout. John ran over, throwing his mask aside as he ran. He bumped into the rail alongside the dugout, but stuck out his glove for the ball. The impact of the ball carried him right on over the rail and he tumbled head over heels down the incline to the concrete runway some four feet below.

Everyone thought he was killed—and all the A's rushed down to help him, the doctor among others. When John started to get up the Doc held him down saying:

"Take it easy, old man, take it easy. You're all right!"

Meantime while John was fighting to get to his feet Collins trotted home after the catch and Cobb tore all the way to the plate from first base. Those two runs would have whipped us, and of course we all squawked. It was a play that wasn't covered by the rules, and after a conference with the other umpires, Tommy Connolly ruled that Collins' score should be allowed, but that the other runner would have to go back to third base. Grabowski, he ruled, had made the catch outside the playing field and had been the victim of unintentional interference into the bargain.

But what a catch it was! Cy Perkins, the Athletic catcher, made one almost as good a season or two previously when he tumbled into a field box at the Yankee stadium. He skidded around on his ear considerably, and lost a lot of skin, but he held the ball for a third out that retired the side and eventually won the ball game.

One of the prettiest defensive plays a catcher can make is the snap throw to first base to catch a runner. I think a base runner never feels so foolish as when he is picked off first base by the catcher. And some of the boys are experts at it. The best man I ever saw at this particular play was Sam Agnew, the old catcher of the St. Louis Browns. I don't know whether Sam invented the play or not, perhaps he did. But he certainly was an expert. He could snap that ball down there like nobody's business, and it was a pretty clever and daring runner who got more than two yards away when Sam was behind the plate.

The advantage of such a play, of course, is that it saves the pitcher and enables him to concentrate more on his pitching and less on the base runner. Luke Sewell of the Cleveland Indians is one of the best present day catchers at snapping a throw to first base. In the course of the season Luke picks off twenty-five or thirty runners in that way, and more important than that, he holds the others so close to the bag that stealing is cut to a minimum.

In holding men on bases you know, or in running bases, the jump from first base to second is the important one. As the ball players figure it, a man on first base isn't so dangerous. It generally takes two singles to score him from there. But once he gets on second base he's in scoring position. That's why pitchers and catchers make so much more effort to stop a man from stealing second than they do from stealing third. And that, too, is why a catcher who is an expert on the snap throw is a mighty valuable man. Benny Bengough of the Yankees is another catcher who has the snap throw down pretty well, though I don't think Benny is as clever at it as Luke Sewell.

The one thing a good catcher must have is nerve! He, more than any other man on the team, must block the runner—and blocking a runner when he's coming in full tilt with spikes threatening takes a lot of real nerve. The old idea used to be that a catcher had to be a big, strong oversized fellow in order to stand the gaff of holding up a pitcher and blocking runners. That's bunk.

Some of the greatest catchers in the business are fairly small men. Muddy Ruel of the Washington Senators is a little fellow. Yet there are few better catchers in the league than Muddy. I think he's the most accurate thrower I've seen since I've been in baseball, and he has the trick of blocking a runner, too. When you come sliding into Muddy at the plate you're lucky if you can get even a corner to touch—and if the throw is accurate Muddy will nail you nine times out of ten.

Benny Bengough and Ray Schalk are little fellows, too. So is Gordon Cochrane of the Athletics. Cy Perkins isn't very big either, and Mike Gonzales, while he's tall and rangy, is built a good deal like a bean pole. He hasn't much weight. Yet they're all mighty good performers, and disprove the idea that catchers have to be big, bruising fellows to hold their jobs.

One of the things a young catcher has to look out

for is getting out of position. The catcher if he's on his toes will back up plays at first base, so long as there's nobody in scoring position. But a lot of the boys carry the thing a little too far, and go straying down the third base line to back up plays there. When they do that they're in trouble.

Heine Zimmerman, the old Giant and Cub third baseman, will go down into history as having pulled one of the greatest boners of all time in the 1917 world series when the Giants played the White Sox. Heine, you may remember, in the final game chased Eddie Collins across the plate with the run that won the game and the series for the White Sox. Of course it was a funny thing to see. The big, lumbering Zimmerman trying to catch Collins, who was as fast a runner as you'll find in baseball. And Eddie made it better by laughing over his shoulder as Zim made a wild dive to put the ball on him. And Heine Zimmerman through all the years has been the goat on a play that wasn't his fault at all.

The real goat on that play was the Giant catcher, who, instead of covering the plate, came rambling down the third base line, leaving the path to the plate alone and unprotected. Once Eddie was away, Zim had no one to throw to. The catcher was out of position and he could do nothing but take up the chase that was hopeless.

The moral of course is plain enough. When there's a possible scoring play on, it's up to the catcher to stick to that plate like glue. It's his job to protect it—and the minute he starts rambling around the lot he's making a mug of himself and his whole ball club.

I've seen a lot of good catchers in my day. Bill Carrigan of the old Red Sox, who was catching when I broke into the league and the man who caught the first big league game I ever pitched, was a great one. So was Eddie Ainsmith. So was Steve O'Neill, who used to be at Cleveland, and is now with the St. Louis Browns. Steve had real baseball instinct. He was what the boys call a "smart catcher," and in his prime he was fast, too. In recent years he has put on weight and the old legs have begun to buckle a bit. He has lost a lot of his stuff. But he still can think with the best of them, and he's a mighty good man to have back there when a young pitcher is in the box.

I think the best catcher I ever saw, though, was little Ray Schalk of the White Sox. Ray had everything. They tell a story to the effect that when Ray first joined the White Sox, Commy wouldn't give him a chance.

"Why you're too little," Comiskey said. "Those big fellows out there will break you into small pieces."

"That, Mr. Comiskey," Ray replied, "is my worry!"

And once in the game he proved that a little fellow is as good as anybody if he knows his stuff. Schalk had everything it takes to make a great catcher. He had speed, and judgment and nerve. He has a great throwing arm, and he never gets nervous or rattled. And he can hit pretty well too—which is always a good thing.

Before the old White Sox got mixed up in that scandal they were one of the greatest ball clubs I ever saw on the field, and Ray was as good as any of them.

CHAPTER X

BASEBALL always has been and always will be a game demanding team play. You can have the nine greatest individual ball players in the world, but if they don't play together the club won't be worth a dime.

Two things make for real team play. The first is players' knowledge of each other that comes from constant playing together. It's this knowledge which is lacking on all young teams. That's why old-timers shake their heads when anyone talks of pennant winning with a team that is made up of young ball players. The second means of whipping play into teamwork is by means of signals—"signs" we call them in the big leagues.

Everyone who ever played baseball knows about signs—but there are mighty few amateur clubs that know how to use them. Either they go along, hit-or-miss with no signs at all, or else they swing to the other extreme and get so many signs that no one can remember them all. Lot of folks think that big league ball players have signals for everything they do. That's bunk. As a matter of fact, a big league ball club has very few signs—but the ones they have they use.

Take for instance the signal between the catcher and pitcher. I can remember as a kid catcher at school, using so many signs that we didn't have fingers enough to go around. We had every curve labeled. One finger, for instance, would be an in-shoot; two fingers, an outcurve; three an outdrop; four, a drop; five, a fast ball—and after that we'd start in on the other hand and have signals for that one, too.

In big league baseball the catcher and pitcher usually have three signs. One for a fast ball; one for a curve; and one for a pitch-out. On a curve ball sign the pitcher may throw a "hook" or he may throw a slow one or screw ball. There's no difference made between curves in the big leagues. Even a freak delivery like Wilcy Moore's "sinker" is thrown on a fast ball signal. As a matter of fact, Wilcy's fast one is always a sinker. It's a "natural," as the boys say.

The pitch-out sign is an important one. The catcher who is on his toes is always watching the opponent's bench and the coaches for possible signs. If he thinks the opponents are putting on a hit and run or a steal, he calls for a pitch-out, which simply means that the pitcher tosses a ball wide of the plate, where it is impossible to hit. If he has caught the signal right and the play actually is on, the base runner naturally is caught flat footed and thrown out. When a catcher knows that the pitcher has great control and can "come in there" with the ball whenever necessary, he uses the pitch-out a great deal. "Wasting one," we say.

The greatest danger of the pitch-out is that the pitcher will get himself in a hole and possibly walk the hitter as a result. With a pitcher who is inclined to be wild anyhow a pitch-out is a mighty dangerous thing. That's something the catcher will have to figure out as he goes along.

Very frequently fans, watching a ball game, will

see a base runner start with the pitch. The batter stands with the bat on his shoulder and the runner is thrown out by a city block.

"Oh what a bum!" the fans say. "What a bum!" and they boo and jeer the runner all the way back to the dugout.

Sometimes of course a runner is caught flat-footed like that when it's his own fault, and he deserves the boos. But nine times out of ten on a play like that, you can mark it down that the catcher caught a hit-and-run signal and ordered a pitch-out. Being caught wasn't the base runner's fault at all. He was just out-smarted by the catcher.

The pitcher and first baseman have a set of "signs" for throws to first base in an effort to catch a runner. The importance of such a sign is two-fold. In the first place the first baseman is in a better position to judge the lead a runner takes. And in the second place each knows what the other is doing and has his head up all the time. There's less chance for throws getting away or going wild and letting the runner advance.

One of the prettiest plays in baseball is to see a pitcher catch a runner off second. It isn't worked as much as it used to be, but you still see it occasionally. That is done by means of signals between the pitcher and shortstop or second baseman. That one usually is a word signal, since the infielders are behind the pitcher who can't, ordinarily, turn around to get a glove signal.

The infielders watch the lead the runner is taking and if he thinks there is a chance to nab him, he works the word signal into his line of chatter. Then he starts for the bag on the sign. The pitcher, standing with his back to the play, gets the signal and starts counting to himself: "one-two-three!" On the count three he whirls and throws direct to the bag, and by the timing of the count the man covering arrives with the ball set to make the play.

It's a play that requires a lot of practice to perfect, and the count of course has to be varied for different men. The shortstop might be especially fast in getting over, and in that case the pitcher probably would throw on a "two" count. Or perhaps he's slow in covering in which case the count might be extended to "four." The first few times it's tried you're apt to see a few balls go rolling into center field, but after practice a team can get it down pat and make it one of the strongest plays in their whole defensive list. So far as the pitcher is concerned his part consists simply in this. "Be sure and get the count right and in turning to throw, make the throw direct to the bag—don't pay any attention to the infielder. He's supposed to be there.

It's important too, in building team play to have the infielders know what the pitcher is throwing on each pitch. But you don't need signals for this. Either the second baseman or shortstop is in position to see the catcher's sign, and he in turn can tip the rest of the players off to it.

Urban Schocker is a wizard on that second base play, and Bob Shawkey is another pitcher who used to pick men off second without missing often. Washington uses the play a lot—and they were particularly good at it in the days when Bucky Harris and Roger Peckinpaugh were the second base combination. These two players have a great sense of timing, and always seemed able to start for the bag at just the proper moment to make the play, yet not too soon to tip the base runner off to their intentions.

A thing that can make a team look either great or rotten, is the way they back up plays on balls hit to the outfield. The idea is to get as many men into each play as possible, in order to prevent a throw from getting away, and if a club is properly coached there will be four men lined up to protect the throw-in on every hit to the outfield.

The shift of the various players, of course, depends on where the ball is hit and where base-runners may be at the time. The best way I know of to show how shifts are made on throws is by a series of charts. My art work isn't so good, but what it attempts to show is Okay. With a single to right for instance, with nobody on, you will note that the second baseman moves over and out toward the ball, the shortstop comes in to cover second, the third baseman shifts a little to the right of the bag and the pitcher goes over back of third base. On a ball hit to left field where the play is at second the shortstop goes out toward left for a possible relay, the second baseman covers the bag, the first baseman moves over toward second and the catcher moves down the first base line.

Each play has its own shift, but the important thing is that whenever possible there be four men always in line with the throw, with the cut-off man always ready to cut the throw and divert it to another base if he sees the opportunity.

For instance there's a man on second and a man

on first and the hitter singles to right field. Naturally the runner on second will try to score on the play, and the right fielder's first thought when he gets the ball, will be to throw to the plate and try and cut off the run. The minute the ball is hit the second baseman cuts out to short right, the first baseman digs in to a spot about ten feet in front of the catcher on a line with the throw-in, and the pitcher goes around behind the plate to back up the catcher in case the ball goes through.

In that case the first baseman is the "cut-off" man. He watches the speeding runners, and he watches the ball. As the throw comes in he senses that it's just a split-second late to nail the man at the plate, but he sees that there is a chance to get the runner going to third base if he makes the play properly. So, instead of permitting the throw to go on to the catcher he takes it or "cuts it off" as we say, and whirls to throw to the third baseman and nail the other runner going to third.

That's the so-called "cut-off" play, and it can be worked on any sort of hit, though the cut-off man may be either the shortstop, the second baseman or the first baseman depending on the play.

That particular play, incidentally, was invented

THE COACHES

by John McGraw and the late Hughey Jennings when they were playing with the old Baltimore Orioles, and it came near revolutionizing baseball. The Orioles worked it a hundred times in the course of a season, before the other clubs got wise. And in the 1922 world series Frisch and Bancroft made the Yankees look like suckers on it no less than three times. The whole success or failure of the thing of course, depends on the good judgment of the "cut-off" men who must decide in an instant whether to "cut-off" the throw or let it go on through to the plate or the base.

In the development of team play the most important man in the business is the coach who watches the scrap from the bench on defense, and occupies the base line coaching boxes when the team is at bat.

It's a funny thing about coaches. When ball clubs first began to send men down the baselines, there was no idea in mind of using him for giving signs or directing play. He was out there to rag and annoy the opposing players, and particularly the pitcher. "Jockeying" we call it now—or taking the other fellows for a "ride."

Some of the things the old-time coaches used to

say, and some of the names they used to call their opponents were terrible. They'd begin with "Bum" and "cut-throat" and "Robber" and go steadily up from there. And if they could get their victim to talking back to them they were more than pleased. For the minute a player begins talking to an opposing coach he's lost. That takes his mind from the game and he's ripe for a killing.

The coaches, out there on the lines, are the fellows who are in best position to grab an opposing team's signals and tip them off. Then they can see the flight of a ball, and are in a position to guide and direct the base runner.

A lot of smart stunts have been pulled on the coaching lines.

One of the best yarns I ever heard, was a stunt pulled by Miller Huggins when he was manager of the Cardinals.

The Cards were mixed up in a tough, tough game, and opposing them was a young pitcher, who for that day at least, seemed to have everything. Inning after inning he went along, setting the Cards down in order, until Hug was almost licked. Finally along in the seventh inning the Cards got a runner to third with two men out. A weak hitter was

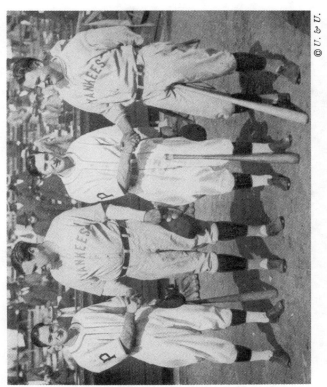

© U. & U.

WHEN SLUGGERS MEET! PAUL WANER MEETS THE BABE FOR THE FIRST
TIME, AND BROTHER LLOYD WANER EXTENDS THE GLAD HAND TO LOU GEHRIG.
PICTURE TAKEN AT THE FIRST GAME OF THE 1927 WORLD SERIES

Wide World Photos

BABE FINISHES A HOME RUN IN THE 1927 WORLD SERIES. EARL SMITH, PIRATE CATCHER, IS WATCHING THE FLIGHT OF THE BALL

up and Huggins, coaching along the third base line, knew very well that he couldn't hit.

Hug was thinking fast, and as the kid pitcher wound up and started to pitch, he yelled from the coaches' box:

"Hey you, let me see that ball!"

Without thinking, the kid turned and tossed the ball over to Hug, who promptly stepped aside and let it roll to the bench. The runner on third scored standing up, and the ball game was won.

Right there was one kid pitcher who learned a lesson. From that day on he surrendered the ball to nobody but the umpire, and then only after strong urging.

John McGraw, of course, is one of the greatest coaches in the business. John directs not only the important moves of a game, but all the details. He pulled one on me in the 1923 world series that I won't forget for a long time.

It was in that wild eighth inning of the final game in which we won the series. Art Nehf had been going great guns for seven innings but in the eighth you may remember, he developed wildness. He walked three men in a row and finally was taken out and Rosy Ryan put in.

To make a long story short I came to bat with runners on second and third, one out, and a run needed to tie or two to win. What a spot to be a hero. But it wasn't my hero day.

Ryan was curving every ball and after "whittling," he carried the count down to three and two. I thought he was going to walk me sure, and I was rarin' to sock it. If I ever wanted to hit a ball in my life that was the time.

McGraw stopped the game and came to the edge of the dugout and called Hank Gowdy the Giant catcher over to him.

"Go out there and tell Ryan to throw this one into the dirt," he ordered. "Ruth is so anxious to hit he'll swing at anything."

And Ryan did just that!

The ball hit the dirt in front of the plate and I swung for a third strike. Afterward when I found out what McGraw had ordered and how he had crossed me up, I was fit to be tied. But luckily for us, Bob Meusel smacked one for a single and we won the game and the series anyhow. If we hadn't I'm afraid there would have been murder done around the Polo Grounds.

In the old days coaches used to spend a lot of time

trying to steal the catcher's signals and tip off the hitters. Old Chief Bender, the Indian pitcher who used to be with the Athletics, was one of the best signal stealers in the business. So was Harry Davis. And many a time they both helped the A's win a ball game by grabbing the other boys' signals and tipping their own hitters off as to whether it would be a "hook" or a fast one.

But that has gone out in recent years. In the first place it's dangerous business. If a batter is tipped off that a curve ball is coming and he gets set for it, and then the pitcher sends up a fast one, the hitter is apt to get his chin torn loose from his undershirt. More than one player has been hit in the head because the coacher thought he had the pitcher's signs and then found out he was wrong.

In the present age the chief signal stealing that is tried, is the effort to discover the batting team's hit and run, and sacrifice and base stealing signals. Those of course, are valuable things to know, and if you can grab them successfully you've got two strikes on the other fellow before he ever steps up there to the plate.

But the boys are pretty cagey, and it isn't easy to steal 'em, anymore. Usually a club has five or six different sets of signals, and they're apt to switch five or six times in the course of a game if they think their opponents are getting wise. And then, if you think you have the signs and haven't you're in an awful fix.

CHAPTER XI

Cobb is game's greatest natural hitter—Is master of style—A few Cobb yarns—Swing hitters and choke hitters—Importance and weakness of each style—Gehrig's hitting style—What makes him great—Willie Keeler's motto—The value of waiting—Correcting batting faults.

THE greatest natural hitter I ever saw is Ty Cobb.

There may be fellows who can hit the ball further, and there are other chaps perhaps who may excel him in some particular department of hitting. But for all around class up there at the plate Cobb stands alone.

I never saw Hans Wagner nor Napoleon Lajoie or the other old-timers who loomed great as hitters. Perhaps they were as good as Ty. Some fellows claim they were. But personally I don't believe it. I don't believe there ever was another one like Cobb, or ever will be.

To young fellows, anxious to learn how to hit, the best advice I can give is simply this: "Watch Cobb. Study his stance, his swing, his timing and his follow-through. Imitate him. Copy his manner. He comes as near being perfection as any batter in the world."

Ty and I have had our little battles. There have been times when only the interference of other players kept us from coming to blows. Once in Detroit, a couple of years ago, we were prime movers in a playing-field row that lead to a near-riot and resulted in a ball game being called in the eighth inning because the police couldn't clear the crowd from the field.

We were rivals and playing-field enemies even in my pitching days. And I pick Cobb as the greatest natural hitter I ever saw, despite the fact that personally I found him easy to pitch to. A pitcher, over the course of his career, runs across certain players who are easy victims, and others who hit everything he offers regardless. Despite the fact that Cobb was and is a great hitter, I always found him easy to pitch to. I can name a dozen men in the league who gave me a lot more trouble than Ty up there at the bat. Joe Jackson was one. Sam Rice was another. Eddie Collins was still another. But despite that I still consider Cobb the king of them all when it comes to hitters.

SWING HITTERS AND CHOKE HITTERS

I'm paid to hit home runs. In a way that's a handicap. To hit home runs I've got to swing from my heels with all the power in my body. Which isn't good batting style. And the greatest tribute I can pay to Ty Cobb is simply this. If I wasn't expected to drive the ball out of the lot every time I come up there to the plate I'd change my batting form tomorrow. I'd copy Cobb's style in every single thing he does. And I'll wager right now that if I could do that I'd increase my batting average 100 points over the season.

Every man in the big leagues has his own individual batting style. But in a general way you can classify batters into two divisions. One is the "swing hitters." Those are the fellows who grasp their bats at the end, take a toe hold at the plate and take a full swing at the ball with all the power they can muster. They're the chaps who bust the fences and send the outfielders back to the wall. They're the fellows who do most of the striking out too.

The other division is the "choke hitters." These are the men we call "smart hitters." They choke their bats, stand flatfooted and take a half swing. They poke the ball, rather than hit it—and while they don't get as much distance as the swing hitters, they are much harder to fool. The choke hitter may not hit many home runs, but he doesn't strike out much either.

When I broke in to the league "choke hitters" were in the majority. Cobb was in his prime then. So was Collins. New players copied their batting styles as much as possible. Then, too, pitchers in those days were permitted to doctor the ball and use all sorts of freak stuff. A fellow had to choke his bat, take a short swing and be prepared for anything, or else he "whiffed." In these days "choke hitters" are giving way to "swing hitters." Change in pitching rules, coupled with the fans' demands for long and heavy hitting has brought about the change.

Some folks say I was responsible for the development of "swing hitting." Maybe they're right. The minute I started hitting home runs with any frequency the newspapers took it up. The fans liked to see the ball go sailing out of the park. After the old time pitching battles, hitting of that sort was something of a novelty and a relief. Other fellows, particularly the big, burly, powerful chaps, began taking their bat at the end and "swinging from the heels" as the boys say. And "swing hitting" came into prominence.

LONG DISTANCE SLUGGERS

Understand I'm not saying hat "swing hitting" is a good thing. I don't think it is. The average kid or man, trying to improve his hitting, will do well to forget home runs and adopt the "choke style." But just the same swing hitting is quite the rage in the major leagues today.

Among the fellows who are "swing hitters" will be found most of the sluggers. I'm a swing hitter. So is Lou Gehrig. So are Harry Heilmann, Goose Goslin, Pie Traynor, Bill Terry, Cy Williams, Tony Lazzeri, Bob Fothergill, Bob Meusel, Rogers Hornsby, and a score of other long distance sluggers whom I might mention.

Not all of us have the same style however.

When Lou Gehrig and I were in the midst of our race for home run honors I had a lot of people ask me which of us hit the ball the harder. I don't imagine there's a lot of difference in the force with which we hit the ball. The point is that we hit differently.

We're both "swing hitters" but there the resemblance ends. I use a golfing swing—loose and easy with a slight upward motion. Lou hits stiff-armed. Lou stands with his feet farther apart, and takes a comparatively short stride with his swing. I stand with my feet fairly close together, the right foot a little further in than the left, and take a long stride with the swing. Lou hits with his shoulders. I hit with my entire body coming around on the swing. Naturally, with my whole body on a pivot I get a longer follow-through than does Lou, whose follow-through is limited by the reach of his rigid arms.

Swinging stiff-arm, too, Lou usually hits a ball on a line. The hardest balls he hits are those which travel say twenty or twenty-five feet above the ground and on a line to the outfield. Any time he lifts a ball into the air (a fly ball) he loses some of the power. The balls I hit most squarely and with most power are apt to go high into the air. My home runs, for the most part, are usually high flies that simply carry out of the park. That's because I take a loose swing with a slight upward angle.

Incidentally that ability to hit a high, hard fly has earned me a lot of home runs in my career. Particularly in Washington and Cleveland where the right field wall is fairly short but marked by a fence that's perhaps sixty feet high. When I hit a ball hard it clears the fence. When Lou really smacks one, the ball takes such a low tangent that it usually bounces back off the fence and is held to a single or a double.

Yet he may have hit the ball every bit as hard and as squarely as I did.

You can prove that by the records. Look up Lou's record and you'll see that he has had very few home runs in either Cleveland or Washington. It isn't that he doesn't hit in those parks. Simply that he's what we call a "line hitter," and a good high fence is tough for him.

Harry Heilmann has a stiff arm swing much like Gehrig's, while Goose Goslin takes a long free swing with plenty of follow-through like mine. Harry, though a right hand hitter, hits to right field a lot. That's because he swings "late." And by swinging late he overcomes, in a great measure, the handicap of being a "swing hitter." Harry is harder to fool than the average "swing hitter." Simply because he swings late, he's not so much a "goat" for change of pace stuff.

The "choke hitters" include such men as Cobb, Joe Sewell, Muddy Ruel, Joe Dugan, Earl Combs, Mark Koenig, the Waner boys, Paul and Lloyd, and Sam Rice of the Washington Senators. Mighty cagey boys they are too—striking out seldom and usually rating right up to the top in the matter of total base hits for the season.

Men like Joey Sewell and Earl Combs rate among the best stickmen in the business. Combs doesn't get a lot of credit for his hitting—perhaps because he happened to be on the same club with Gehrig and myself, who get drives so much longer. But he's one of the best hitters in the game just the same. And one of the most dangerous men in a pinch, that a pitcher is ever called upon to face.

Like Heilmann, Combs is a "late" swinger—and being a left handed hitter, he usually hits to left field or center. Combs is smart, however, and can "cross up" a pitcher by some pretty nifty place hitting. And the ability to place hits is the real mark of batting prowess. Willie Keeler, one of the greatest and most scientific little hitters who ever lived put his finger on the whole thing one day when someone asked him the secret of hitting:

"Hit 'em where they ain't," Willie replied.

That sounds simple enough but it isn't so easy. To understand what is meant by place hitting you must understand first that pitchers are always striving to make a man hit in a certain direction. The place hitter is the chap who can take a ball which, ordinarily he would hit to right, and hit it to left, or vice versa.

PLACE HITTING

The greatest example of place hitting I ever saw was put on by Ty Cobb one afternoon at the Yankee Stadium a couple of seasons ago. Ty was taking batting practice and some of the boys on our bench were kidding him.

Shocker, in particular, was "on" him.

"Hey, Ty" Shock yelled. "You're supposed to be good. Let's see you hit one down the right field foul line."

Ty took a half swing and planted the ball within three feet of the spot Shocker called for.

"Now hit one to left," Shocker commanded.

Ty socked one a mile a minute over third base.

"Center field, now," Shocker ordered.

Ty dropped the ball over second base.

"Well, I'm a son-of-gun!" Shocker exploded. "Let's see you foul one back of the catcher."

Ty did it, too.

"You win," Shocker said, "I'm whipped."

Ty grinned. "That's nothing," he shouted to the Yankee bench "you think you're quite a guy—suppose you catch this one." And Ty drove a foul right into our dugout, so close that Shocker could almost have reached out and caught the ball.

That's real place hitting. But it was no accident.

A lot of times, when the boys got on him a bit during batting practice, I've seen Ty stand up there at the plate and drive a ball right into the dugout sending all the fellows scurrying for cover.

Of course, hitting like that in batting practice, and doing it in a game are two different things. Just the same Mr. Cobb comes about as near being the perfect place hitter as anyone we have sticking around the league today.

Eddie Collins is another chap who hits where he wants to hit, rather than in the direction the pitcher wants him to. One of the pet hitting stunts of these two is to fake a swing and find out whether the second baseman or shortstop is going to cover. Then, when they've found out, they lay one down right through the position that's vacated as the man goes over to cover second. That's putting on the hit and run with a vengeance.

Personally I'm not a place hitter. No "swing hitters" are. I'm big and strong and get a lot of drive back of the ball. Everyone knows that nine times out of ten I'll hit to right field. But if I really get hold of one it doesn't make any difference whether the fielders know where it's coming or not. It just goes out of the park.

HITTERS BORN NOT MADE

Just the same, I like to try a bit of place hitting once in a while and in the past two or three seasons I've got so I can hit to left pretty well by choking my bat and taking an extra step forward with my swing. Naturally when I choke my bat the opposing fielders can see what I'm going to do—but I get away from that by not choking until the minute I start my swing. Then they don't have time to come over for me.

I don't believe it's possible to make a hitter.

A fellow either can hit the ball, or he can't—and that's that. But it is possible for a natural hitter to improve, and it's possible to overcome a hitting weakness.

The batting eye, and the sense of timing are born in a man. If he hasn't got them, there's no way of giving them to him. But mechanical things can be overcome by practice. The swing, the stance, the stride—these are things that can be changed and improved.

Every batter who comes into the big leagues has his "groove." That's the place where he likes a ball best. With some fellows the "groove" is a ball through the middle. With others it may be a high ball outside, or a low ball inside, or vice versa. Given a pitch in that particular spot he can whale the tar out of it.

By the same argument every player has a hitting weakness. Perhaps it's a curve ball. Perhaps it's a change of pace. Perhaps it's a low one inside. The pitcher is trying constantly to pitch to that weakness and keep away from the "groove." The hitter, of course, is trying to hide his weakness and get the pitcher to pitch to his strength.

A hitting weakness is one thing that can be overcome by constant practice and hard work. When I first broke into the game I had a tough time hitting change of pace pitching—particularly the real slow stuff. I swung too fast, and either fouled the ball off into the stands or missed it entirely. Today I believe I can hit the slow stuff about as well as any "swing hitter" in the business. And all because I worked hard at it. I used to go up to the batting cage during spring practice and have the pitchers give me slow ball after slow ball. I'd swing and swing until I was arm-sore. But I got my timing down so I could hit the slow ones—and that was the thing I was after.

Another thing that used to bother me was over-anxiety to hit. Most fellows suffer from that at one

PROPER BATTING STANCE. FEET SLIGHTLY APART, WEIGHT EVENLY
DISTRIBUTED, BAT WELL BACK FOR A QUICK SWING

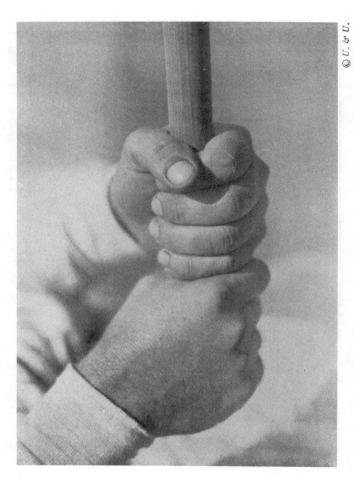

THE PERFECT GRIP FOR A SWING HITTER. A CLOSEUP OF THE WAY BABE RUTH HOLDS HIS BAT

THE VALUE OF WAITING

time or another. You're so anxious to hit that you swing at bad balls. The toughest thing anybody has to learn is to keep that old bat on the shoulder on the "close ones." The smart pitcher is always working the corners, keeping the ball just an inch or two outside or inside, a mite too high or a bit too low. The over-anxious hitter is duck-soup for that sort of pitching.

Most fellows go up there to the plate with the wrong idea. They see a ball coming up on the corner and they think to themselves: "This one looks pretty good. I'd better swing at it or maybe the umpire will call it a strike, anyhow."

What they ought to think is:

"That one's not good enough. If I let it go chances are it will be called a ball."

You may get crossed up and have a strike called now and then, but you'd be surprised how often it really is a ball. And once a pitcher sees that you're not to be fooled on those "almost strikes" he'll come in there with it and give you something a little beter to hit at.

I learned my lesson in that 1923 world series. I've already told you about it. It was plain over-anxiety to hit that made me swing at a ball in the ground for that third strike that Ryan threw. Since then I've been a little more careful.

Of course there's danger the other way too. As Umpire Bill Byron used to say, "You can't get a hit with the bat on your shoulder." That's true enough. But neither can you get a hit if you keep swinging at bad balls all the time.

As I started out to say, it's possible for a fellow to improve his hitting, and correct his hitting weaknesses. The answer is practice, hard work, and confidence. When Lou Gehrig first came into the league he couldn't hit a low ball inside. Lou did two things. First he changed his stride. He had been stepping well into the ball. Now he stepped just a little straighter. Then he practiced, and practiced. Today not many pitchers have the nerve to pitch 'em low and inside to Lou anymore. He has overcome his weakness.

Rogers Hornsby, one of the greatest right hand hitters the game has ever known, is another chap who had to work hard when he came into the league. Strange as it may seem Rog was no bargain with the stick when he first came into the league. But he had the natural hitting eye, and Miller Huggins, who was then manager of the Cardinals, set him to work. First off he changed his stance, took a little of the stiffness out of his legs and taught him to stride with the swing. Then he got him to loosen his shoulders a bit—and the first thing anyone knew Roger was tearing the hands off infielders who got in front of his drives.

I guess there's no better curve ball hitter in the big leagues today than Joe Harris, who starred with Washington and later with Pirates. Joe socks that old curve ball for sleeper jumps right regularly. Yet when he came into the league Joe couldn't hit a curve ball. He simply studied the thing out, discovered what was wrong and corrected it. It takes a long time, sometimes, but it can be done.

Nobody can put down a set of rules for correcting batting.

In the first place no two men hit alike. When I was a kid in Baltimore, playing on a kid team, we had a young fellow on our club who thought he knew a lot about baseball. He started out to make us all into hitters, and his theory was that the most important thing was swinging on a straight line. So he took two boards and nailed them on a post, leaving just space enough between them for a bat to pass easily. Then for fifteen or twenty minutes at a time we'd stand up there and swing at that opening, the idea being to develop a swing that would keep the bat moving in a straight line. It sounded fine but it didn't work out. The first thing we knew we were all swinging perfectly stiff. If a ball happened to come through the middle of the plate, waist high, we would murder it. But if it was high or low we were sunk.

Here are some general rules that might be worth following:

If your weakness is a fast ball, don't hold your bat quite so far back on your shoulder. Shorten your back swing and shorten your stride. In other words speed up a little.

If your weakness is a curve ball, change your stride to step into the ball a little more. Most fellows who can't hit curve balls are chaps who stride out of line or "pull away" from the ball.

If you have trouble with the slow stuff choke up your bat and start your swing a bit later. Most batters who have trouble with slow ball pitching are "pull" hitters. That is, they are meeting the ball "out front."

And whether your difficulty is a slow one or a fast one a curve or a change of pace; whether you're trouble is a high one or a low one, inside or outside, the most important thing of all to remember is simply this.

"Don't hit at the bad ones. Make 'em be in there." In a poker game the wise guy always remembers the old saying: "You don't have to look." In baseball, up there at the plate, it's well to remember always:

"You don't have to swing!"

CHAPTER XII

WHEN Al Simmons first broke into the American
League a lot of the wise boys predicted that he
wouldn't last out his first season.

"He steps in the bucket" they said—meaning
that when he takes his stride his left foot (Al is a
right hand hitter) pulls away from the plate.

"A sucker for a curve ball" the pitchers told each
other. And then tried him out. Al promptly
knocked their curves to all corners of the lot—and
he's still doing it. And stepping in the bucket, just
the same.

Which just goes to show that there's no rule
governing the good hitter. I don't think there's
another man in either league who could stand at

the plate the way Al does, and still hit the size of his hat. But stepping in the bucket is Al's natural hitting form—and what is natural is generally best in baseball.

Al overcomes that back step by using an exceptionally long bat—the longest in the league I think, and just as long as the baseball law will allow. The result is that he can reach the outside corner for a curve if he has to, and at the same time he's far enough away that the inside stuff doesn't bother him.

Understand I'm not recommending that all hitters "step in the bucket." And I'm not holding Al's hitting form up as an example. I'm just illustrating the point that there's no rule governing the good hitters. There's no one more off form, than Al, and mighty few better hitters. It all goes back to the same thing.

The most important thing about hitting is to be natural, and be easy.

George Burns, the Cleveland first baseman, is another hitter whose stance at the plate is entirely off form. George stands perfectly straight, with his feet right together. There's no other man in either league who stands that way. Even if they tried it the chances are they would be a complete bust. Yet George hits—and hits well. And what is more he hits most any sort of pitching.

Joey Sewell has always appealed to me as about the ideal type of left handed hitter. Sewell stands up there flat footed, feet fairly far apart and firm set in the box. He takes his swing from the shoulder, putting his body into the pivot only at the last minute. The result is that he's a hard man to fool. The strikeout records prove that. For the past three or four seasons Joey has struck out less than any man in the league. One season he went through 154 ball games and struck out only three times. A fellow like that is a real hitter.

Sewell hits a ball hard and far too. He doesn't get his body into the swing like the "swing hitters" do, but he does get a lot of wrist snap. If you've ever taken any golf lessons you know how the golf pro coaches you to use your wrists. Hitters of the Sewell type use the same sort of wrist snap when they hit a baseball. Tony Lazzeri is another chap who gets most of his drive from his wrist. Tony used to be a boiler maker, and constant use of the heavy boiler-maker tools plus the arm exercise has developed his forearm and wrist muscles to the limit. Tony really is built slight and to look at his hands you'd never dream of their power. His fingers are long and tapering, his palms are narrow and almost girl-like. But he has a wrist and forearm like steel. That's what gives him his driving power at the bat and his snap throw from second.

No ball player ever made good either as a hitter or a fielder unless he had well developed wrist and forearm muscles. There are a lot of exercises that can be used to get that development.

One of the common methods used by ball players to strengthen the wrist and forearm is to buy a five or ten cent rubber ball, and carry it around, gripping and relaxing it all the time. If you do that for fifteen or twenty minutes a day you can strengthen the forearm a lot—and if you don't think those muscles get a real workout by gripping, just try it. The first fifteen minutes of that exercise will make your arm ache clear to the elbow.

Earl Combs uses this method. Earl had a bad throwing arm when he came into the league, but gripping exercises have strengthened his wrists and his throwing has improved a lot.

I never had any trouble that way myself. My

arms and wrists and shoulders have always been well developed. If anything I'm a little "top heavy," and the thing I have to watch most is my legs. I've learned a lot of things in the past two or three years, among others the value of proper exercise. For the last three winters I've worked out regularly in a gymnasium, and there I've spent most of the time on exercises that would develop my legs and keep my waist line down at the same time.

One of the common faults of kid hitters particularly, is that they don't use the proper bat. Most of them try to swing bats that are too heavy, figuring of course that the heavier the bat, the more distance they can get. That's wrong. Any time a player uses a bat that feels heavy in his hands, he's making a mistake. The ideal bat is one that balances perfectly, one that can be swung with the same easy, smooth motion with which you swing your arms. A too heavy bat requires a jerk to start on it's way, and once underway it requires additional effort to direct it's course. Naturally that makes a jerky, choppy swing. Not so good.

The average weight of bats used by big leaguers is 36 ounces. The bat I use is much heavier, but you must remember that I'm a pretty big boy. And I'm cutting down on bat weight as the years go by. A few seasons ago I used a 54 ounce bat, long and with the weight well at the end. Now I'm using a 46 ounce club—and each season when I have a new set of bats made, I have an additional ounce taken off.

The longest bat in the big leagues is swung by Al Simmons. I've already told about that. The shortest bat I ever saw in my day was used by Whitey Witt—a stubby club with a thick handle. The reason for that was, that as a lead off man Whitey's business was to get on base. He bunted a lot, and a thick handled bat gave him a chance to get hold of balls thrown inside.

I don't know who uses the lightest bat today, but Wally Schang, the old Yankee catcher, uses one of the lightest. Alongside my bat, Schang's looks like a toothpick. Earl Combs uses a light bat, too. Rogers Hornsby is another chap who uses a fairly light model. So does Sam Rice of the Senators.

Now and then some player will come along with a freak bat of some sort. Like the old bottle bat that Heine Groh used to use. So far as I can see there's nothing to that sort of thing—except perhaps in the mind of the man using the bat. If some freak stick will give him confidence, why it's a good thing. After all confidence is one of the biggest things in hitting.

All big leaguers have their favorite bats. For years I used a big black model that the boys called "Black Betsy." I had the same identical thing in several other "sticks" but somehow that black one had a little more appeal. And I used it for the better part of three seasons before it finally broke on me.

Players often trade bat models, but they guard their pet bats as if they were solid gold. Earl Combs is one of the easiest going, most pleasant even-tempered chaps I ever saw. But once last summer I saw him when I think he would gladly have committed murder—all over a bat.

Earl had a pet stick that he had been using all season long. He protected it like a child, and he wouldn't even use it in hitting practice. "That bat is full of basehits," he would say, "and there's no need wasting them on hitting practice."

One afternoon Hug sent Mike Gazella up to hit just as batting practice ended. Mike didn't look around to select a bat, just took the first one that came handy. It happened to be Combs' pet club. On the second pitch Mike swung with everything he had and broke the bat square in two. I thought Earl would crown him. I never saw a man get any more angry for a few minutes than Combs was— and for two weeks after that he couldn't speak to Mike without making some crack about that bat.

A few years ago Sam Crawford, the old Detroit outfielder and slugger, sent me a sample bat from the coast. It was one of those trick things made out of four separate sections, pasted and fitted together. Sam wanted me to try it out and see how it worked.

The first time up I hit the ball over the fence for a home run and during the entire game I got myself two doubles and a single in addition to the home run. Naturally I was tickled pink. In the clubhouse that night I had Woodie send Sam an order for six of the bats.

They came along a few days later, and Colonel Ruppert happened to be in the clubhouse when they arrived. He took a peek at the bill and threw his hands in the air. Those bats were listed at six dollars each.

"Well, Ruth," the Colonel commented, "I guess

we keep these bats in the safe, eh, with the mortgages and family jewels."

The funny part of it all is, that a few days later some manager protested that the bats were illegal —since they were made of four separate pieces of wood. As a result the umpires ruled them out, and so far as I know the good Colonel still has those six bats stored away "in the safe with the mortgages and the family jewels."

Harry Heilmann gave me a bat a week or so before the season ended last year. It was one that he had been hitting with, and he liked it. "Try this out in the world series," he told me, "it's full of base hits. There's only one provision though," he added. "You're not to use it against the Detroit club."

Ball players are always trading bats. Goose Goslin never comes to New York that he doesn't come over to our dugout and look over all the bats. Wallie Schang is another one who is always looking for "good wood." And very frequently a couple of players will get together and trade bats like little kids swap stamps for the collection albums.

The best woods for bats is either ash or hickory.

BATS

Both are tough hard woods with plenty of "spring" (elasticity). The hickory is a little heavier than the ash. For myself I usually use hickory, but most of the boys prefer ash. In buying a bat, the chief thing to look for is a smooth even grain.

Joe Dugan for years has used a black bat of Cuban wood—a soft light weight wood. Joe likes a light bat and he figures that the Cuban makes up in "spring" what it may lack in weight. And he certainly can drive a ball with it, you have to hand him that.

But when all is said and done, confidence is the biggest thing in hitting . Fellows who go up there to the plate with a lot of confidence are pretty apt to hit.

Fellows get queer notions in hitting. They have superstitions about their bats: they have superstitions about certain pitchers. Hitters will tell you in all seriousness that certain pitchers have their number, or that certain other pitchers are always easy.

Late last season I started a stunt which gave the boys quite a laugh for a time. I started "notching" my bat for home runs, like the old gun-men used to notch their guns when they killed a man. Everytime I would hit a home run I would cut a notch in the bat handle of the club I had used. At first the boys began laughing, but as September came around and I started hitting all sorts of pitching for home runs they changed their tune.

I have one bat in the club house that has seven notches in the handle, and another one that has eleven. Eleven is about as many as a bat will hold for the minute you start notching the hitting surface the umpires will throw the bat out. The whole thing started as a sort of "kid," and as a matter of fact I wasn't superstitious about those notches at all. But most of the gang thought I was. And I did accomplish one thing. By putting those notches in the bat I identified my own clubs and the other fellows would leave my bats strictly alone.

Speaking of funny customs there's the old, old habit of "boning" bats. Fellows were doing it when I came into the league, and I suppose they'll still be doing it fifty years from now. "Boning" a bat consists in rubbing it with a bottle or a bone or some hard smooth substance of that nature. The idea is that such constant rubbing smooths the surface, fills in and contracts the wood pores on the surface and prevents breaking. I've seen fellows sit for hours at

WHEN RUTH SWINGS, HE SWINGS ON HIS TOES, AND FINISHES
WITH HIS WEIGHT ON HIS LEFT FOOT. HENCE HIS TREMENDOUS
DISTANCE

© U. & U.

GEHRIG IS A SWINGER OF THE FLAT-FOOTED TYPE. HE THROWS
HIS WEIGHT FORWARD, AND FINISHES HIS SWING ON HIS RIGHT
FOOT

a time boning away at their favorite bats. Some of them stain the wood as well. Frankie Frisch never chews tobacco, but he used to use tobacco to rub his bat with—working it into the grain until the bat looked as though it had been stuck in some tobacco vat. The umpires don't permit that any more— but "boning" comes within the law, and everyone does it.

One other thing while we're on the subject of hitting. All hitters have different styles. Some swing flatfooted, others take a long stride. Some choke and some swing. But there are certain features in which all hitters—if they're good ones—act alike.

They have to have perfect balance, perfect timing and a good eye. Balance and timing are much the same. It is timing which enables a man to meet the ball at the exact instant when all his body is thrown into the swing. It's timing which enables a man to hit fast and slow balls with equal ease. It is timing which, more than any one thing, is the secret of real hitting.

And the unfortunate thing about it is that timing is one thing which you can't teach. It's born into a man. You either have it or you haven't. Little kids, starting to go to singing school, are the same way. Either they have a musical sense or they haven't—and if they haven't they never acquire it.

All forms of athletics depend on timing. It's the secret of golf and handball and tennis. It's the secret of boxing, and it's the secret of football offense. A few years ago I saw Red Grange run for three touchdowns against the University of Pennsylvania eleven. And the thing that impressed me most was not his speed, or his power. It was his timing. It was so perfect that he could avoid tackles by the split part of an inch. His timing was so perfect that in going through the line he always managed to reach his hole at the very instant when it was open widest. And that is timing developed to the last degree.

Go out to the ball game some day and watch the really great hitters. You'll notice that they don't seem to swing any harder, or with any longer arc than the poorer hitters. But they have perfect timing sense. That's the most important thing in batting.

As I said before, a man either has a sense of timing or he hasn't. But you can improve you're timing. Lots of times I go into slumps, as do all other hitters. The first thing I look to is my timing. I try swinging a bit later, or a bit earlier.   I shorten or lengthen my stride.   I experiment with every angle of timing.   And usually I can correct my fault, even though I may not know exactly what it is.

CHAPTER XIII

Hits are valuable in so far as they score runs—Levsen pitches
two hit game and loses—Real test of hitting is ability to
smack ball when hits mean runs—The danger of "tightening up"—Hitting slumps and how to overcome them—
Bunting, its value and use—Great bunters and how they
operated—The bunt attack and how it is put over.

BASE hits look fine in the batting averages, but
they pay off on runs scored.

All the base hits in the world are wasted if the
hitter doesn't complete his journey and check in at
the home plate with a run. Funny things happen in
baseball, proving that hits are just as valuable as
you make them.

Back in 1926 in a game against the Cleveland
club the Yankees got just two hits off Emil Levsen,
the Cleveland pitcher. Only two men got to first
base—but both of them scored, and we won the
game 2 to 1. A little later in the season, with Tom
Zachary of the Browns pitching against us, we
accumulated the healthy total of 11 hits together
with five bases on balls. Yet we didn't score a

single run and were shut out for the first time that season. Every one of those men were left on base.

Look at the left-on-bases figures and you can get a pretty good line on the offensive strength of a club. For men left on bases are the tip off on poor batting. Every man left on base is an opportunity lost and anytime a club has eight or ten or more men left it's a pretty sure sign that something's wrong with the team's attacking power.

The real test of hitting greatness is the ability to step up there and hit when a hit will mean runs. "Hitting in the pinches" we call it—and it's the most important part of the batting game. Lou Gehrig, during the 1927 season, drove in 175 runs for a new record. In other words Lou came through when there were men on bases. He did his best hitting when we had runners in scoring position.

I've heard a lot of pitchers say, and they've told me to my face, that they'd rather pitch to me in a pinch than to Gehrig.

"You either knock the cover off the ball or strike out," they say. "We've got a fifty-fifty chance with you. But this Gehrig is dangerous when there are runners on the bases."

Tony Lazzeri is another one who can pound that

ball, when hits count. Tony had an odd record during the 1926 season. He hit only .280 for the year, and he struck out more times than any other player in the league. Yet he drove in 147 runs that year and rated second in the league in that department. In other words, he did this hitting when hits counted. He was a much better and more dangerous hitter than his batting average showed.

One of the chaps I'll remember longest is Eddie Foster, the old Washington third baseman. Eddie never rated as a real star, and there were scores of other players in the league who were considered more dangerous and better men with the stick. But Eddie certainly was my personal poison. He hit everything I ever pitched—and hit it plenty. And when it came to a pinch, with runners on bases and a ball game hanging in the balance, I would rather pitch to Cobb, Speaker and Crawford in a row than throw to Eddie. He ruined many a ball game for me over the period of three or four seasons.

I don't know why it is, but it's an established fact that some fellows are at their best in a pinch, while others seem to go to pieces at such a time. Take Joe Dugan for instance. Joe isn't what you'd call a heavy hitter. He seldom hits for extra bases and I suppose most clubs look on him as one of the weaker men in the Yankee batting order. But put Joe in a crucial series, or turn him loose in a world series and he's deadly poison. Joe has played in three world series with the Yankees and he has never yet failed to star out in the field and at bat. He's just a natural born "money player" as the boys say —and plays his best when the going is toughest.

Joe Judge is another hitter of that type. Goose Goslin will outhit Joe in the averages by 20 to 50 points. But with runners on bases and a hit needed to win the ball game most pitchers would rather pitch to Goose a dozen times over. Earl Combs is a good hitter in a pinch. Rogers Hornsby is a corker. Joey Sewell is another mighty tough one.

Theoretically hitting in a pinch is no different than going up there with nobody on and two out. Actually there's a lot of difference. With nobody on the base, the hitter has a clear and easy mind. He doesn't have to worry about protecting the runner. He doesn't have to keep his eye peeled for signs and signals. And more important than that, he doesn't have anybody to worry about but himself. He can give his whole and undivided attention to hitting.

With runners in scoring position it's very different. There are a dozen things to watch—but more important than all these is the sense of responsibility. The average hitter "tightens up," he stands stiff at the plate, his muscles tighten and his whole motion is jerky. When he does that he's gone. The batter who stiffens up and loses his easy, free swing is an easy victim for a pitcher.

The same thing happens when a hitter goes into a batting slump. And every hitter has them. No matter how great a hitter he may be there will come times when, to use a common baseball expression, "he can't hit a barn door with a bull fiddle."

And ability to get out of a slump is another test of the real hitter. Some fellows claim that a slump doesn't bother them. That they take it as a matter of course, knowing that they will work out of it sooner or later. That's bunk. There never was a ball player lived who could go through a batting slump without worrying. It's simply a question of how much you worry, and whether or not your worry is about the slump or over methods of overcoming it.

The worst part of a batting slump is that it affects a man's play to the field too. As long as the base-hits are coming regularly the average ball player is sitting on top of the world. He has pepper and enthusiasm. Everything is fine. But when the old slump comes along everything is upside down.

Smart managers realize that. One of the best lines I ever heard pulled came from Miller Huggins a couple of years ago. We had a kid infielder in camp who looked as though he would burn up the league. He was pounding the cover off the ball— and digging everything out of the dirt that came his way.

All the newspaper writers were enthusiastic and wrote red hot stories about this latest find who would show up any infielder in the league.

"That kid is the best I ever saw," one of them said to Huggins one day, "why you're all set now. You don't have to worry any more."

Hug grinned, that slow, funny little grin that he has.

"Maybe so," he said. "I hope you're right. But before I commit myself I want to see how he acts after he has gone through seven or eight games without a base hit."

The kid who was going to burn up the league, is back in the minors now. No one ever hears anything about him. The slump that Huggins spoke about came, and he went all to pieces. He was one of those nervous sort of fellows who just worried himself out of the league over base hits that didn't go safe.

The worst part of a hitting slump is that a fellow will hit the ball all right—but always at somebody. When you're in a hitting streak it seems that everything you hit falls safe. When you're in a slump nothing goes right. You hit 'em on the nose and the ball goes right into some outfielder's hands. You lay down a grounder that nine times out of ten would be a basehit, and some infielder does a Houdini and comes up with the ball for a putout.

I get many letters from amateur players each year, asking what to do to get out of a batting slump.

That's a problem. I guess no two fellows use the same methods.

Personally I change my batting style. I experiment. I change my swing and my stance. I try stepping forward a bit in the batting box. I change to bats of different weight.

With me, I've found that the best method of overcoming a slump is to choke my bat and start "choke hitting" for a while. I reduce my stride to a minimum and stand as flatfooted as possible. Naturally that shortens my stride, and I "push" instead of "pull" the ball. And most of all, I try to worry as little as possible about it.

Sometimes when I'm in a slump I'll catch myself tightening up with the pitch. When I do that I simply call for time, and step out of the box, until I can get squared around and loosened up again. Here's another thing you've got to watch when you're in a hitting slump. The longer you go without a basehit the more anxious you are to get one. As a result of the anxiety you're more than apt to swing at bad balls, simply because you're too anxious to hit.

When I'm in a batting slump one of the first things I do, is start taking that first one. It isn't always easy. When a chap wants a base hit badly it's tough to stand up there and watch one go shooting across the corner and not swing. But it's a wise move—for it curbs that over-anxiety and keeps you from hitting at bad ones. Once a fellow starts swinging wild he's sunk—and his slump will come to an end somewhere in Oshkosh or Cedar Falls.

The business of getting runners around the bases is one of the most scientific departments of the game. And there's no set rule for attack. When

187

I first broke into baseball most of the clubs were using the old-fashioned sacrifice and steal game. In recent years play has switched, and the steal has more or less disappeared. Clubs today depend more on the hit-and-run.

But as I said before there's no set rule you can follow. It depends on the sort of club you have. Miller Huggins for instance has always favored what he likes to call "smart baseball." He likes the sacrifice attack. He likes the steal. But he doesn't use it because he knows such an attack wouldn't work so well with a club like the Yankees. We're sluggers for the most part—and have to score our runs by hitting power. We haven't any great base runners. Meusel and Combs can steal with the best in the business but they're only two.

We have few fellows on our club, too, who can handle the sacrifice properly. The Yankees, for the most part, are "swing hitters" and hitters of that type never will shine at the sacrifice game. Knowing these things Huggins forgets his "smart baseball" ideas and makes the most of the type hitters he has. Which is good baseball. George Moriarity, over in Detroit, on the other hand, uses the steal a lot. He has a bunch of fast, speedy, youngsters who know how to run bases and the steal with them is the best form of attack.

The Washington Senators are long on the sacrifice. Most of the men on their club can "lay them down" to perfection, and do it. John McGraw has always favored the "hit and run" as a means of advancing his runners and bringing in scores. But just the same that didn't keep John from changing his tactics to a base-stealing game when he had that team of speed boys back in 1912 to 1916. Even yet they talk of the way the Giants "stole the pennant" during those years.

After all it comes back to the same proposition. The method of attack depends on the club—and the smart manager uses the form that is best for his individual group of players.

There's no play in baseball any prettier than the bunt when it's properly executed. But not all ball players can do it. Watching from the stands it looks easy. But it isn't. In the first place smart pitchers have all the good bunters card catalogued. And nine times out of ten when a fellow starts to bunt he finds the pitchings coming through high, fast and inside, which is the toughest spot in the world for a bunter.

To be a bunter a fellow has to have a keen eye. He has to have speed in getting to first, in order that he may beat the ball. And more important than that he not only has to hit the ball, but he has to hit it to certain limited places. The bunted ball that goes direct to the pitcher is worse than a strike-out. The bunt that is hit too hard and rolls fast down the line to an infielder; or the one that is hit too easily and lands in front of the plate for the catcher to grab—these too are worse than no bunt at all.

If you can't put the ball where you want to, say eight times out of ten, then you'd better not try any serious bunting where there's a ball game hanging in the balance.

One of the best bunters I've ever seen was Whitey Witt. Whitey had a wonderful way of laying that ball right down the third base line, and being fast getting down to first, he could beat them out. Whitey used to get from twenty-five to thirty-five base hits a year on bunts.

I remember a line Whitey pulled in the clubhouse one afternoon toward the end of the 1923 season. Whitey had about 32 hits on bunts to his credit, and some of the newspaper men were talking to him about it.

"Yet," he said, "I'm conservative. I believe in saving distance. Those thirty-two hits, laid end to end, would just about equal one of Babe's shortest home runs. Yet he got only four bases on the distance and I got thirty-two. Science pays, my boy, science pays!"

Poor old Whitey is out of baseball now and raising tomatoes down on his farm in Jersey. We see him every now and then and occasionally he puts on a uniform and works out with the boys when we're home. And he can still "Lay 'em down," even though his legs have gone back and he can't run much any more. I guess it's a knack, that once acquired, never leaves a fellow.

From what old timers tell me Willie Keeler must have been about the king of the bunters. I never saw him—but I've heard plenty of stories about his ability to lay them down in any direction. Miller Huggins, the manager of the Yankees, is another chap who was a wizard at the bunt game during his playing days. Seems as though little fellows always make the best bunters. Usually they're pretty fast which is a big asset. And the fact that they're so small makes them hard to pitch to. Pitchers can't work on them as carefully as they do on a bigger fellow.

In baseball we divide bunts into two classes. There's the ordinary roller down the third base line which is just a "bunt." Balls pushed toward first base we call "drag bunts." And when you can catch the infield playing back the drag bunt is a mighty good weapon for a left hand hitter. Properly placed it pulls the first baseman off the bag, and is out of reach of the pitcher.

Somehow there doesn't seem to be so many good drag hunters now as there used to be. One of the best of the lot was Ross Young, the old Giant right fielder who died recently in San Antonio. Ross had that drag bunt down to perfection, and could drive a first baseman nutty with it. He used it against us in the world series a lot—and even such a veteran as Wallie Pipp had trouble making a play on it.

Charley Jamieson, of the Cleveland Indians, and Earl Combs of the Yankees are about the best drag bunters in the business today. Combs I think is even better than Jamey, because he's faster. And speed is a mighty big item in a drag bunt play. Sam Rice, the speedy Washington outfielder, is another

THE END OF EDDIE COLLINS' SWING. NOTE BAT IS CHOKED AND WEIGHT IS RESTING ENTIRELY ON BACK FOOT. COLLINS, LIKE RUTH, USES A LONG FOLLOW THROUGH

THE BABE CHANGES HIS STYLE FOR A BIT OF CHOKE HITTING. NOTE CHOKED BAT AND FLAT-FOOTED STANCE AT THE END OF THE SWING. ALSO SHORTENED FOLLOW-THROUGH

batter who can drag the ball down the first base line plenty. But Sam doesn't use the play as much now as he did a few years ago, when he was batting in leadoff or second position in the batting order.

Of course you've got to pick your spots for a bunt attack. A poor fielding pitcher is always a sucker for such a play. I've already told how Alan Sothoron was bunted right out of the league. Managers are also quick to use the bunt when they've got a new third baseman working against them. Unless a third baseman can come in and handle bunts he's not much use—and in the big leagues we're quick to test out a man on that particular job.

Handling bunts is one of the places where Joe Dugan used to shine brightest. Joe is the best third baseman I ever saw at coming in and scooping the ball with one hand, then throwing to first while still off balance. Fellows around the league used to say of Joe that he could throw better and more accurately when he had both feet off the ground than he could when he was all set for a peg.

And that's about right. Joe makes bad throws occasionally, but nine times out of ten they come when he has plenty of time and gets all set. He very, very seldom throws wild, on one of those quick "scoop and throw" plays.

The bunt has two purposes. First, it's to upset the infield and get the hitter safely to first. Second, it's used as a sacrifice, in which case the object is to advance a runner even at the cost of sacrificing the hitter. The two plays are entirely different. The fact that a man is a good bunter, doesn't always mean that he is a good sacrificer.

On the sacrifice the idea isn't so much to avoid a play as it is to so place the ball that a play is possible only at first base. If the runner to be advanced is on second, then the bunt must be so placed that the third baseman will have to come in and handle it. If the runner is on first, the best place for the sacrifice bunt is midway down the third base line so the pitcher has to handle the play. Or, in the case of the left handed hitter, a drag bunt that pulls the second baseman in to cover first base, is always good.

CHAPTER XIV

Waiting 'em out!—Frank Chance puts one over—Jamieson
smacks the first one—Not always easy to wait—Trying
to outguess the pitcher—The intentional pass—Putting on
the hit and run play—Eddie Collins a master at it—Huggins expresses an opinion.

How often, when you go out to the ball game, you
hear the voices of the coaches echoing above all the
noise and cheering.

"Wait him out!" "Make him pitch! Make it be
in there!"

Those are sort of stock phrases in baseball,
phases that the coachers use constantly. And they
contain pretty good advice, too.

A waiting attack has been the downfall of many
a pitcher—and it's particularly effective against a
pitcher who is inexperienced or one who is inclined
to wildness. Of course you have to pick your spots.
Playing a waiting game against a fellow like Alexander, for instance, is right in his groove. His
control is so perfect that the minute a team starts
to wait him out they're putting themselves in a hole.

The waiting attack, of course, is very simple. It consists merely in not swinging until forced to. Batters, playing that sort of a game, will take two strikes without moving the bat from their shoulders. And its purpose is two-fold.

The first purpose is to make the pitcher work as hard as possible. Fellows who swing at the first ball are giving the pitcher all the best of it. In that sort of an attack a pitcher can get through an inning with pitching only three or four balls. Against a waiting attack he has to pitch at least nine even if every thing he pitches is a strike.

The second purpose of a waiting attack is to take advantage of a pitcher's wildness. With a lot of pitchers, if the hitter has patience enough to wait and wait, he eventually will draw a base on balls— and a base on balls is just as good as a basehit both in getting men to first base and in advancing runners.

In this day of slugging the old waiting game isn't played as much as it used to be. Bill Carrigan used to tell a story of Frank Chance when he was managing the famous old Cubs. Chance, Carrigan said, won a crucial game in a pennant series by waiting tactics. At the start of the game he instructed every. man on his club to wait.

CHANCE PUTS ONE OVER

"Don't swing at all," Chance warned. "Just go up there and stand. If you're called out on strikes it's all right."

And for six innings the Cubs did that very thing. For six innings the opposing pitcher, pitched hitless ball—for not a single Cub hitter took his bat from his shoulder. But in that time the pitcher averaged twelve to fifteen pitches an inning.

Finally in the seventh inning, Chance suddenly switched his tactics.

"Go up there and smack that first ball," he instructed.

The Cubs did just that. A couple of base hits came in a row. The pitcher upset by the sudden switch, lost his stuff. He grew wild. And in one inning the Cubs put over four runs and won the ball game. That's carrying the waiting attack to the last degree—and such methods aren't favored much these days.

But the waiting game is still mighty important in baseball.

To some hitters, waiting comes natural. Others can't seem to withstand the temptation to swing at that first one if it's "in there." Pitchers soon catalogue hitters and pitch accordingly. Mike Gazella and Pat Collins of the Yankees for instance, are waiters. I've seen both Pat and Mike take two strikes time after time without so much as offering to swing at the ball. Charley Jamieson of the Cleveland Indians, on the other hand is a first ball hitter. A pitcher can put that first one over with safety to either Pat or Mike, but putting the first one over to Jamieson is murder. He'll sock it for a city block.

In modern baseball teams are apt to change their attack two or three times in a single game. Perhaps for an inning or two they will wait the pitcher out. Then they may suddenly shift to a first ball hitting attack. Midway of the game they may shift still another time. The idea is to keep the pitcher guessing.

After all baseball is a game of guessing and out-guessing. A lot of hitters carry the idea too far. They try to out-guess the pitcher on every pitch. Personally I'm opposed to guess hitting.

"How do you know when to expect a curve ball and when a fast one?" I guess I'm asked that question a hundred times a year. The answer is that I don't. The minute a fellow starts in trying to guess the pitch he's just wishing trouble on himself. For there's nothing in this world more upsetting than being set for a fast ball and then have a curve come looping up. And there's no better way in the world to get a trip to the hospital with a cracked head, than getting set for a curve and then have a fast one come swinging in at your chin.

After all there's only one answer to be made to the young fellow who is asking constantly for advice as to how to hit.

The answer is: "Pick out a good one and sock it!"

I've talked to a lot of pretty good hitters in the past ten years and I've watched them work. Go over the list from top to bottom—Hornsby, Goslin, Heilmann, Gehrig, Traynor, Cobb, Judge, Bottomley, Roush--there's not a "guess" hitter in the lot. They all tell you the same thing.

"I never think about whether it's a curve or a fast one that's coming. I simply get set—and if the ball looks good, I sock it."

As a matter of fact half of the time when a fellow gets hold of one he doesn't really know whether it was a curve or a fast one he hit. A slow ball, naturally, he can recognize—but the others he can't. The crack of the bat just naturally drives all question of curve or fast one out of your mind. Many times I've cracked out a homer, and when I got back to the bench I've had some of the boys ask me what it was I hit. And I couldn't tell them. All I knew was it was over—I liked it—and I swung just right.

That day in 1927 that I got my sixtieth home run off Tom Zachary, the left hander with the Washington Senators. Naturally there was a lot of interest in it, and the newspapers next day carried stories as to the sort of ball I hit. Some of the writers said it was a fast ball inside; some of them said it was a curve ball. Some of them thought it was high outside, and others thought it was low inside. A few said it was a fast ball right down the middle.

It wasn't any of these. The ball I hit for my sixtieth homer was a screw ball—a slow ball that comes up with little or no rotation and broke in and down, being thrown by a left hander. As a matter of fact I didn't know at the time whether the ball was inside or outside. In fact Manager Huggins and I agreed later that it was on the outside corner. Zachary, however, insists that the ball was slightly lower than waist high, and on the inside. Tom should know. All I can say for certain is that it was a screw ball, and that it looked good to hit!

CALLING THE PITCH

I always get a great kick out of newspaper stories in which the boys try to tell the sort of pitch that batters hit for base hits. It can't be done. From the press box or the stands it's mighty hard to see a curve ball any time, even when the batter has his bat on his shoulder. Once he starts to swing and the bat comes between the observer's eye and the ball, it's twice as hard if not impossible. When you consider that a lot of curve balls are hit before they start to break, or at the very moment they start to break, you can appreciate just how hard it is for the man in the stands to tell what sort of ball is pitched.

The tip off on that, I think, is the fact that a certain National League manager, watching Pipgras pitch in the second game of the 1927 world series, commented at some length on Pipgras' "excellent curve that had the Pirates guessing." As a matter of fact George pitched fast balls almost exclusively that day. I don't think he threw a dozen curves during the entire game. Now I ask, if a veteran manager, trained to watch, and sitting in the stands can't be sure what is being pitched—what chance has a casual observer to call the turn. It simply can't be done.

It's like fans along the third base line trying to judge balls and strikes as they go zipping across the plate. And that's next to impossible.

But I started out to talk about the waiting policy. As I said you find certain hitters who are natural born waiters. They're fellows who have such keen eyes and judgment that they can judge a ball to the fraction of an inch. "Hard to fool" the pitchers say. Such players are mighty valuable fellows to have around. Very frequently, in baseball, a couple of bases on balls may be the entering wedge for a batting rally. In a game in which the pitcher has been breezing along, the boys on the bench are as pleased to see him give a base on balls as they are to see a base hit. For a base on balls frequently is the first tip-off that comes on a pitcher weakening.

Once a pitcher shows signs of weakening is the moment to bring the old waiting game into play. The Yankees last year beat Lefty Groves of the Athletics four straight games simply by waiting him out. Lefty is a great pitcher—but he's inclined to wildness and after he's sent that fast curve in there a few times without the hitters offering at it, he begins to get nervous. Or I should say did—for Lefty is older and more experienced now and the things that upset him when he broke in don't bother him any more.

I guess there is nothing in baseball that has caused more discussion in recent years than the intentional pass. Fans have howled and wailed about it, and they've demanded some sort of penalty for an intentional pass—but nothing has been done. Probably nothing will be either, for the intentional pass has a place in baseball. I've been the victim of the intentional pass as much as anyone in either league I guess, and I've howled and complained with the rest of them. But all the same I can get the pitcher's viewpoint, and it's a good one. He isn't out there to please the crowd. He's out to win ball games—and if passing one hitter to get at another will win, why he's within his rights in doing it.

You will notice that last season I wasn't passed nearly as often as in the seasons before. The reason is, that with Gehrig coming up, it wasn't good baseball to do it. Giving a man an intentional pass is just like handing the enemy a scoring chance—and that's penalty enough for the pitcher.

Then too there are certain situations arise which make the intentional pass good baseball, regardless. Suppose there is a runner on second base, one out, and the score tied. A fairly good hitter is coming up, followed by another one equally good. In a spot like that an intentional pass might be a wise move. For by passing a man to first you "block the bases," that is you make a force play possible at both second and third and pave the way for a double play which would retire the side without scoring. With a runner only on second a double play is virtually impossible.

The intentional pass is not particularly costly in a case like that. The man on second will score on a single anyhow, and the fellow who is passed to first can't possibly go all the way round on a one-base hit. Intentionally passing a good hitter to get at a weak hitter also is good baseball, despite the wails of the fans who want to see base hits.

I've seen pitchers pitch to a hard hitting catcher and have him break up a ball game, instead of passing him to get at the weak hitting pitcher. And fans up in the stands are apt to say "Well he had nerve anyhow. He pitched. You've got to hand him that."

Hand him nothing! All I hand him is that he was too stubborn to do the thing he should. He gets no credit in my book at all—and remember that

THE HIT AND RUN PLAY

I have suffered much from this intentional pass business. What I'm trying to point out is that baseball is a game of strategy, and a lot of things which may not please the folks in the stands are mighty good baseball just the same.

One of the greatest offensive plays in use today is the "Hit and run." That's just what the name implies. The runner starts with the pitch and the batter hits the ball, on the ground and behind the runner if possible.

Suppose there is a man on first base and nobody out. The hit and run signal is flashed. As the pitcher starts his motion the runner dashes toward second. The hitter swings, striving if possible to hit the ball between first and second base, back of the fleeting runner. The advantage of course is that by prearranged signal which tells the runner just what the hitter will do, the runner is enabled to get a long lead and can advance an extra base. Or, by having that long start, he avoids the possibility of a double play and reaches second base safely even though the runner may be thrown out.

The fact that a man is a good hitter doesn't mean that he will be a good man on the "hit and run." Here again hitting style enters into it. The choke hitter is always the best hit and run man—and the "swing hitter" very seldom is able to put on the play successfully. That's because the choke hitter is better able to place the ball where he wants it. "Calling his shots" the boys say.

With the hit and run play on the man at the bat usually shortens his stride and eases up on his swing. That's because he's got to make sure of hitting the ball. Failure to hit the ball, on a hit and run play, means almost certain death to the runner—and hitting the ball, unless it happens to be a hard liner direct into an infielder's hands, is practically a guarantee that the runner will reach his base safely.

Eddie Foster, the old Washington third baseman, was one of the best hit and run men I ever saw. Eddie could come as near laying that ball midway between second and first as any man in the business. The only chance of breaking up the hit and run play with Eddie up, was to "waste" one—and pitchers don't do that unless they are pretty sure they have the other fellow's sign.

A lot of men in the league now are good on the hit and run. Eddie Collins is a wonder at it. Ty Cobb was a great one. Sewell of the Cleveland Indians is a wizard on the play. Hitters who seldom strike out always make the best hit and run men—regardless of whether they hit the ball far or not. Joe Dugan is as good on the play as anyone we have on the Yankees. And Bob Meusel can put it on well, despite the fact that he is both a right hand hitter and a swing hitter.

The hit and run play usually demands that the hitter send the ball to right field. Fellows like Cobb and Collins frequently play it the other way. With a man in position for the hit and run they will feint a strike to see who covers second. Then if the shortstop makes the move to cover, they will hit through the shortstop position, sending the ball through the space he vacated to go over to the bag. That's a good play for a fellow who can place hit. But it's a bad gamble for the amateur. For if anything goes wrong, a double play is almost certain—and there's nothing upsets a batting attack like a double play.

The success or failure of a hit and run depends a lot on the type of pitcher who is working too. Pitchers who pitch fast and high are the easiest victims of this attack. A pitcher of the Wilcy Moore type who pitches a low "sinker" is tough. Wilcy makes opposing pitchers hit into the ground, and hitting into the ground on a hit and run is very likely to give an infielder an easy chance for a double play.

Whether to use the hit and run, or the sacrifice to advance runners is a matter for the manager to decide. It all depends on the players. Some clubs are best at one play some are better at the other. Certain other clubs, speedy and fast and shifty, may discard both in favor of the steal.

Miller Huggins, smart manager that he is, covers the subject in this way:

"I'm not interested in baseball theories," he says. "Baseball is one game that can't be run by rule. The team that wins ball games is the team that makes the most of its own mechanical abilities and to thunder with the other team's strategy. Some other manager does things differently perhaps—but he's got a different ball club to do it with!"

CHAPTER XV

The batting order—The kid idea—Getting the most out of
hitting strength—The lead-off man—Combs and Waner
are good—No reason why pitchers shouldn't be good hitters—A few examples—Heaviest hitters bat third and
fourth—That's the scoring position.

WHEN I was a kid playing around Baltimore, we
held to two general rules in fixing our batting order.
There was the old system of starting with the first
baseman and batting around to the right fielder, clos-
ing with the catcher and pitcher. There wasn't anything very scientific in that scheme, but it had its
advantages. It was easy to know who was up and
didn't offer much chance for argument. As a kid I
saw more fights started over whose turn it was to hit,
than for any other single reason I can remember.

The other method of arranging the batting order
consisted in starting with a good hitter, then a weak
one, and alternating right through. The idea of that
was that there would be a good hitter coming up in
every inning to start something. That there would

also be a weak one to ruin anything that was started, didn't come in for much consideration.

Of course arranging a batting order in a kid game is a matter that requires plenty of strategy. Just as the boy who owns a glove and ball is generally pitcher, so is the kid who owns a bat, pretty apt to be first hitter—baseball strategy be durned. At least that was true when I was a youngster, and from what I've seen boys haven't changed much since.

But seriously the batting order is a mighty important thing—and managers consider it very carefully. Just as winning a ball game depends on the runs scored so are the runs scored dependent on the batting order. A manager must figure always on getting the most from his hitting strength, and at the same time covering up as much as possible his hitting weaknesses. And every ball club, no matter how strong, is sure to have hitting weakness somewhere.

If there are no others, there's the weakness of the pitcher as a hitter. Most pitchers are weak hitters. Personally I've never been able to figure out just why. I believe that pitchers as a class, should be able to hit just as well as infielders or outfielders or catchers. The trouble is that most baseball men take the at-

PITCHERS AS HITTERS

titude: "Oh well, you can't expect the pitcher to hit" and let it go at that. Just the same there are a lot of pitchers who can hit well.

"Dutch" Ruether was always a good hitter. George Uhle of the Cleveland Indians is about as tough a man up there at the plate as you'll find anywhere. Walter Johnson always hit well—and Herb Pennock usually comes up with his share of base-hits.

As a pitcher, I always managed to smack that ball fairly well, and, considering the little I played, I hit just as well when I was pitching as when playing the outfield. There are a number of pitchers who, through as pitchers, have made good in the outfield. Reb Russell the old White Sox left hander, is one of them. Joe Wood, the old Red Sox fast ball pitcher, went into the outfield and played several seasons after his pitching days were over. "Lefty" O'Doul, who comes to the Giants this year as an outfielder, with a reputation for real slugging, once wore a Yankee uniform as a pitcher. Joe Bush, the old Yankee pitcher, always could hit —and is frequently used as a pinch hitter.

These pitchers are only a few of many who can hit with the best batters in the business. It only goes to show that the old idea about pitchers not being hitters, is all wrong. The big trouble is that the pitchers don't want to hit. They take the attitude that they're carrying the burden of the defensive work, and that any strenuous effort at the plate or on the bases would injure their pitching effectiveness.

That idea started many, many years ago—when a club carried only one or two pitchers. In those days when pitchers were overworked, it's true that they couldn't afford to expend any more energy than possible at the plate or on the bases. But now a days things are different. With ball clubs carrying eight or ten pitchers, and pitchers called upon to work only every fourth or fifth day, there's no reason in the world why the pitcher shouldn't carry just as much of the defensive load as any man on the club. As I see it there are three reasons why a pitcher rates as a poor hitter.

In the first place he believes it himself. He has listened to the old howl for so long that he just accepts it as fact.

The second reason is that pitchers, being pitchers, are more interested in the opposing pitchers' business than in their own. In other words, when they're up there at the plate they're always trying to "guess" what the other fellow is doing. Instead of getting a good firm stance and swinging at the good ones, they're thinking about whether it's to be a "curve" or a fast one, a low one or a high one. No "guess" hitter ever makes a good hitter.

The third reason why pitchers can't hit, as I see it, is a lack of practice. Hitting requires constant practice. You've got to keep in there swinging. Pitchers on a big league club, get batting practice only on the days when they are scheduled to work —and only a couple of rounds then. The best hitter in the world can't be at his best when he handles a bat for perhaps ten minutes twice a week. But given daily practice and the idea that they can hit, there's no reason why pitchers shouldn't smack that ball just as hard as any other type of ball player. And what a great thing it is for a club to have nine real hitters up there taking their swing, instead of eight batsmen and a pitcher.

But I started out to talk about the batting order. Most big league managers follow the same general scheme in making up their batting order. Naturally the more good hitters they have, the easier is the job, and the less attention they have to give to placing their men. The ideal batting order would be one of nine men—all of them Cobbs or Hornsbys. But that doesn't happen.

Managers, if they're smart, pay a lot of attention to the selection of their first hitter. "The lead-off man" he is called. Here must be a man of good and quick judgment, a player who can hit well, and one who is inclined to be a "waiter." His job is to get on base. It doesn't make any difference whether he gets there by a hit, by walking, or by being socked in the ribs—so long as he gets there.

The mere fact that a man is a good hitter, doesn't make him a good lead-off man. He has to have speed in addition—but most important of all is that good judgment of pitched balls which enables him to force the pitcher to "come in there." As I said before his job is to GET ON BASE—and to MAKE THAT PITCHER WORK ON HIM.

Few lead-off men, if you will notice, are first ball hitters. In nine ball games out of ten, you'll see that first man up "take" the first one without swinging—whether it's outside or right through the middle.

The best lead-off man I've seen since I've been in baseball is Earl Combs of the Yankees. Probably

THE LEAD-OFF MAN

I'll get a lot of argument on that statement, but it stands. There are other men in the league who can bunt better than Earl; there are other fellows in the league who get more bases on balls. There are other lead-off men, though not many, who may have better hitting averages. But there's one thing at which Earl has no equal—and the most important thing of all. He gets to first base safely. Last season for instance, Combs reached first base safely seven times out of every thirteen times he came to bat. Think of that! For every two times he comes to the plate he reaches first once. And that's not counting the times he was safe by reason of having forced some other runner at second!

I'm not up on records, but I doubt if that record of Combs last season has ever been equalled by anyone. And that's why I say he's the best lead-off man I ever saw. He gets on base the most! And once on base, he knows how to get the rest of the way 'round.

The Yankees have been very fortunate in their lead-off men in the past few years. Before Earl Combs came along Whitey Witt held the job, and Whitey was a wizard too. Being little and short he was a tough man to pitch too—and he used to draw a good many passes in the course of a season. But Whitey had one weakness. He could go down to first base like a flash. There were few men in the league who could go faster. But once he reached first he was actually slow. Somehow he didn't seem to have the knack of baserunning.

Lloyd Waner, the sensational little outfielder of the Pirates, is another fine lead-off man. Waner not only is a keen judge of a pitched ball, but his size is in his favor. Little fellows are always tough to pitch too. A lot of managers figure that the lead-off man should be a small fellow—the smallest on the club. I never could see that size made a lot of difference except that little fellows usually are fast, and they present a small target for the pitcher. It's the keen eye that counts most however. Earl Combs isn't small. Neither is Sam Rice of Washington. Johnny Mostil of the White Sox is pretty sizeable, too. Yet they all have been mighty useful lead-off men.

On the other hand there are some little fellows who have rated as stars. Jimmy Sheckard of the old Cubs is one. And Jimmy, deserves to be rated among the really great outfielders of the game. Miller Huggins was small, and a great lead-off man—though Huggins was just about as good batting in second place or the "sacrifice" position. Donie Bush, former shortstop of the Detroit Tigers and now manager of the Pittsburgh Pirates, led off for the Tigers through many a long season and many a tough campaign. And Willie Keeler, the one man whom all critics agree was the daddy of scientific hitters, was a lead-off man through a life time of baseball seasons.

There's one important thing to remember in selecting a lead-off man. Don't waste a real slugger on the job—for the lead-off man gets little opportunity to drive in runs, as compared to other posts in the batting order. The reason for that is simple enough. The tail end of the batting order brings up the catcher and pitcher, and these two, by actual record, get to first base less than any other two hitters on the club.

Take the case of Earl Combs for instance. In 1927 Earl got well over 200 hits during the season; more than any other man on the club. Yet he rated fifth or sixth in the matter of runs driven in. It wasn't because he was a bad hitter with men on bases, either. Just the opposite he's one of the best boys in a pinch you'll find anywhere. But usually when he comes up there is nobody on. His business wasn't to advance other runners for the most part. It was to get on base himself.

Second place in the batting order is looked upon as the "sacrifice" position. The lead-off man is supposed to get on first. Then it's up to the second man to sacrifice him to second where he will be in scoring position. But the practice doesn't work out as well as the theory, particularly in these days of plain and fancy slugging. Nevertheless it's a wise move to have a good hitter batting in second place —and one who can put on either the hit and run, or the sacrifice as occasion may demand. Smart managers are careful to use a "choke" hitter in second place if they have one on the club. That's because the second place hitter is often called upon to put on the hit-and-run and that's a play that is next to impossible for a swing hitter to put over right.

In third and fourth place in the batting order you usually find the sluggers. These are the fellows who are counted on to drive in the runs—the siege guns of the attack as the sport writers call them. They may not have as high a batting average as the fellows who bat second and first, but they're the babies who can be counted on to drive the ball for long distances when they do connect. If they don't get a base hit they've always got the chance of driving out long flies that will score runs, anyhow. Managers of big league ball clubs have differences of opinion on a lot of subjects but they all agree on the value of centralizing their "slugging" power in third, fourth and fifth place in the batting order.

You have only to look at the old box score to prove the statement. In the first world series— the one between Boston and Pittsburgh in 1903— you find Leach and Wagner batting third and fourth for the Pirates and Stahl and Freeman for the Boston club. These were the sluggers doing their stuff then as they do now. And it's been the same all through baseball history. There were Schulte, Chance and Steinfeldt of the old Cubs, Cobb, Crawford and Veach of the smashing Detroit Tigers of twenty years ago. Collins and Baker batted third and fourth for the famous old Athletics, and they were the sluggers of the outfit. Speaker and Lewis were the clean-up pair for the championship Red Sox; Collins and Jackson for the White Sox of 1917; Frisch Young and Kelly for the Giant champions of a few years ago. With the Cardinals of 1926

Hornsby and Bottomley drew the slugging posts of honor and the Pirates of 1927 had Waner and Harris on the job. It all tells the same story. Third and fourth place in the batting order is the spot for slugging strength, and if you have any left over you can send them into fifth and sixth place as well.

Personally I'd rather bat in third place than any other spot on the lineup. That's probably because I'm used to it. And then too, I know that I'm being followed by another man who has a good chance of coming through if I fail. I don't go up to the bat feeling like some sort of a last chance or as though the whole weight of the game was on my shoulders.

I want to say this right here and now too. I feel that a lot of my success in hitting home runs has been due to the fact that I've always had fellows following me in the batting order who were just as dangerous as I was. In 1920 when I got 54 home runs and again in 1921 when I hit 59, I was followed in the batting order by Wallie Pipp and Bob Meusel. Both of them had particularly good seasons, and there wasn't much percentage in passing me to get at fellows like that. Then last year I had

THE SIXTH PLACE

Lou Gehrig coming up after me—and the pitcher who passed me to get at Lou was taking a mighty big chance, believe me. Consequently they pitched to me. They had to.

Here's a funny thing about a batting order that most folks don't realize. Next to the lead-off man, the fellow who is called upon most often to start the inning at bat is the chap in sixth place. And next to the man batting in third place the fellow who bats sixth comes up most often with men on bases. I don't know why that is. I only know it's true! A couple of seasons ago some of the newspaper men traveling with the Yankees got in an argument over it, and one of them went over the scores for a whole season of play to check the thing up. The scores book showed the truth of the claim.

The answer, of course, is that sixth place is a mighty important spot, and requires a man second only to the lead-off man in his ability to get on base. You know in baseball there's nothing so important as getting the jump on the other fellow. And the most important way of getting the jump is for the first man up in an inning to get on first base. If a team is fortunate to have two men who are good at the business of reaching first base the problem is easy. Put one of them in to lead off and bat the other in sixth place in the batting order. Of the two, take the one that is the best slugger for sixth place. The reason for that is that he is more apt to be followed by weak hitters and it's therefort necessary that he be able to hit for extra bases as much as possible since he can't expect so much help from the fellows who follow him.

Which brings us down to the tail end of the batting order, and unless a team is mighty fortunate in having unusual hitting strength that's apt to be the dumping ground. Some managers believe in putting a little of their hitting strength at the bottom, but personally I'd rather see it bunched. Of course if you've got a top-heavy batting order, there will be times about every other inning when your team won't threaten. But just the same I've got a hunch that it's a good idea to have all your dynamite ready for explosion at once, even if you can get around to it only every second or third inning.

Unless the catcher happens to be a very strong hitter and some other player is unusually weak most managers prefer to bat their catcher eighth and the pitcher ninth. It's a sort of custom now—

THE TAIL END

but it has a basis of judgment too. It's simply this. The pitcher and catcher are not in the game regularly, and putting them at the bottom of the batting order breaks up team play the least of any place you could have them. The other six men, batting in regular position learn to know each other's style of play and can make the most of their base hits. And anyhow the tail end of the order is always the weakest and can stand shifting without harm, better than any other place you can name.

CHAPTER XVI

Team work counts—The hit and run, and when to use it—
The squeeze play—Urban Shocker puts it over great—A
bit of advice on base running—Great base runners the
game has seen—Schang pulls a good line on Cobb—The
slide an important feature of base running—Spiking no
longer done—The story of how spiking began.

I'VE seen a lot of ball games in all these years, and
I've had a lot of "kicks" from the game. There's
the kick that comes from making a good catch or a
good throw. And the kick that comes, too, from
hitting a ball and watch it going sailing up and out,
until it disappears over the fence and you hear the
cheers and the applause as you go trotting around
the bases.

But those thrills are all personal.

There's another sort of thrill that ball players
know—the thrill of seeing a perfect play, perfectly
executed. And now, after a lot of years of big
league competition, I've about decided that the two
most beautiful plays the game holds are the perfect
steal and the perfectly executed "squeeze" play that

STARTING THE SLIDE. BOTH FEET OFF THE GROUND AND THE BODY ALREADY STARTING TO FALL

AWAY FROM THE BALL

MIDWAY OF THE SLIDE. LEFT FOOT ALREADY EXTENDED TO CATCH THE PLATE. RIGHT FOOT DOUBLED UNDER AND RIGHT HAND EXTENDED TO BREAK THE FORCE OF THE FALL

THE SQUEEZE PLAY

brings the runner sliding home in a cloud of dust
with the winning run. Somehow there's something
about these two that aren't duplicated anywhere else
in baseball. Maybe it's because they require so much
coördination: because they must be perfect to be
worked at all, and there's always a thrill in doing
a thing exactly right.

I'm sorry neither the squeeze play nor the steal
are used as much now as they were a few years ago.
Slugging, driving baseball has made them unneces-
sary. One run means very little in modern baseball. Most managers play for three or four, and the
squeeze seldom is called into use unless it be in the
final inning or two of an occasional tight game.
The steal too has been more or less passed up for the
same reason. You seldom see a runner steal third
base any more, and a steal of home is practically
unheard of except in the so-called "double steal."

The theory of the squeeze play is simple. It is
used only when there is a runner on third base and
one run needed to tie or win. Suppose, for example,
that it is the ninth inning, the score is tied and the
team at bat has a runner on third base and one out.
The stage is all set for the "squeeze."

The signal is flashed. With the motion of the

225

pitcher's arm the runner on third breaks loose for the plate as fast as he can go. He doesn't pay any attention to the pitcher or the hitter—just runs as hard as he can and throws himself at the plate.

Meantime the batter bunts the ball down the third base line, a slow twisting bunt that's a little too far out for the catcher, and too far toward the third base line for the pitcher. With the proper sort of a bunt the play can't fail to score a run. Since the runner gets such a long start there's no player in the world can handle the ball quickly enough to retire him.

But the bunt must be perfect and there's the catch of it.

Bunting today is pretty much a lost art. The hitter might miss the ball; he might pop it into the air; he might drop it dead in front of the plate. And any of these things are fatal. For the runner once he has started can't turn back. He just keeps coming.

It's a great play, and a beautiful play. And with experienced men working it, it's about as sure a way of scoring as you can find in the book. But there's danger in it too—as in all types of baseball strategy and besides it scores only one run. And as I said

THE SQUEEZE PLAY

before one run in modern base ball doesn't mean much. A few years ago the pitcher who was lucky enough to get a two or three run margin considered the game just as good as won. Today a margin of three or four runs means very little. One bad inning can overcome all that and then some. So the squeeze has about gone out.

The best "squeeze play man" I know of today in baseball is Urban Shocker, the Yankee pitcher. Shock never rated as a great hitter or anything like that, but he certainly can lay that ball down. It's a matter of record that he drove in 11 runs for the Yankees last season. And six of them were scored on squeeze plays, three of which won ball games.

Ray Schalk, the peppery little catcher and manager of the White Sox, is another chap who is a wizard at it. Naturally, when the squeeze play looks probable the infield plays in. The third baseman comes well in on the line and the first baseman moves in on the grass half way to the plate. All of which makes it that much more difficult—but just the same, properly executed, the "squeeze" will work eight times out of ten.

Its success or failure, naturally, depends on the hitter. If he lays the ball down properly the runner from third can score standing up—particularly if he's a quick starter and gets a good lead, plus a start with the pitcher's arm. But the hitter has to hit— and he has to hit on the ground. Otherwise—well, it's just too bad.

The "steal" like the "squeeze play" is used much less than it was a few years ago. A lot of good baseball men say that stealing is a lost art. I don't believe that. There are just as many clever base runners, and just as many fast men in the league now as there ever have been. But the fact is that the steal isn't as necessary. There's no need in a man taking a chance on being thrown out on a steal when any batter that steps up there is apt to plunk the ball over the fence for a home run so he can score standing up.

But just the same we have some mighty fine base runners today, as always. And we have some clubs too that don't have the hitting power and go in for the steal as a real part of their scoring attack. George Moriarity, the old third baseman who took over the management of the Detroit Tigers after years of umpiring, went in pretty strong for the steal in his season as manager, and got away with it. The Tigers as a club, stole more bases than any other team in

either league—yet they're not particularly fast as a team. Johnny Neun probably was the best man they had. I'll never forget a game Johnny played against the Yankees when he stole five bases in nine innings. The first time up he stole second. His next time at bat he walked, then proceeded to steal second and third. And on his third appearence at bat he added insult to injury by getting a single and then stealing second, third, and home, one after the other and on three pitched balls. That's stealing bases—and no old timer in the business ever did better than that. Johnny was the best base runner the Tigers had. But they have other good ones in Tavener and Gehringer, and Moriarity even went as far with the "steal" game that he had Bob Fothergill and Harry Heilmann stepping them off. And those fellows never would break any speed records anywhere.

Base stealing isn't so much a matter of speed as it is a question of catching the opponents off guard, getting a good lead, and then being able to start fast. Players like Eddie Collins and Johnny Neun are fast but not sprinters. Yet they're good base runners simply because they know how to take a long lead, and how to start. I could name a dozen men in baseball who could run rings around Collins over a hundred yard course. But not a one of the lot can get away faster or pick up full speed in so short a distance.

Of course there are exceptions. Johnny Mostil of the White Sox, and one of the greatest outfielders the game ever has known, managed to steal a lot of bases in the course of a year, and on speed alone. But he's the exception.

The greatest base runner who ever lived, I think, was Tyrus Raymond Cobb. Cobb had speed to burn. But he had other things too. He had wonderful judgment plus a hook slide that is the best I ever saw. More than that he was a quick thinker. He seemed able to sense what the other fellow was expecting, and then he'd do the exact opposite. Some of Cobb's base running stunts will never be forgotten. I've seen him score all the way from second base on a dinky sacrifice fly. I've seen him go all the way home from first on a single, and I've seen him steal home more times than I can remember.

I don't know how many two baggers Ty has made in his career, but I'd make a bet right now that at least half of them were singles that he stretched into two base hits by base running cunning and half of his three-baggers, I know, would have been only doubles and skimpy ones at that, for the ordinary base runner.

For twenty years Ty Cobb ran wild through the league, and during the ten years when he was in his prime as a ball player he had every other club in the league nutty. He'd try anything—and get away with it.

One of the funniest lines I ever heard, and at the same time one of the greatest compliments ever paid Cobb came from Wally Schang. It all happened in the secrecy of the Athletic's club house, but it was so good that the other players told it and in a few days it had traveled all around the league.

The Athletics were about to engage the Tigers in a crucial series and Connie Mack was holding a meeting to discuss the games. The boys went over all the Detroit hitters, one by one, and decided how they would pitch to each man. They discussed their own plays, and everything in the baseball category. Finally they came to the matter of stopping Cobb. Connie asked for suggestions but no one came through.

Finally he turned to Schang, who had been with the club only a couple of seasons.

"Now Wallie," Connie said, "suppose the Tigers

were one run behind, Cobb was on second base, and you knew he was going to steal. What would you do?"

Schangie's answer was quick and to the point.

"I'd fake a throw to third then hold the ball and tag him as he slid into the plate."

And he wasn't far wrong at that, either.

As Bob Shawkey used to say "The only things Ty Cobb never stole were first base and the umpire's whisk broom, and he would have had those in another two years."

I've heard a lot of explanation of Cobb's success as a base runner. The best I ever heard was from Cobb himself. And it was short and sweet.

"I've made a success as a base runner because I keep my head up," he said. What he meant of course, was that he was always watching for opportunities. The slightest fumble, the slightest hesitation on the part of an opposing player in handling the ball— these were invitations to Cobb, and he never refused them. Even after some of the speed had gone out of his legs and the years had taken their toll of energy he was still dangerous, simply because he kept his head up and his eyes open. And those two things are the first requirements for a good base runner.

GREAT BASE RUNNERS

Cobb, as I said before, is the best base runner I ever saw and, I think, the greatest who ever wore a spiked shoe. There have been others who have been really great too. There's Max Carey who came into the big leagues way back in 1910 and is still on the job after 18 years of big league service. Carey was a speed boy when he came into the league—but he was intelligent too. And now that his speed has deserted him, he has experience and knowledge to fall back on, and is still able to show the way to most of the fellows in the league when it comes to scientific base running. The secret of Max's success as a base runner is his ability to get a start. Carey watches the opposing defense with the eye of a hawk. He's always set and ready to go—always on perfect balance so he can dash in either direction. And like Cobb, he has a perfect hook slide.

Another great base runner is Frankie Frisch of the Cardinals. Frankie is peculiar in that he uses a head-on slide and is one of the few men in the big league who uses such a slide. Frankie has a good argument too. He says that by sliding head first instead of feet first he saves the split part of a second in getting underway.

Of course these men are not the only great base

233

runners. But they are typical of them all. Sam Rice of the Washington Senators, Bob Meusel of the Yankees; Al Simmons and Walter French of the Athletics, the Waner boys of the Pirates: Eddie Roush of the Giants: Rogers Hornsby, Hack Wilson, Bucky Harris: Bib Falk—these men are all great on the bases.

The greatest slider I ever have seen was Ty Cobb. Ty was the first man in baseball to develop the "hook slide." That, as most everyone knows, consists in throwing the body sideways and catching the bag with the toe. The advantage of the hook slide over the straight slide is that it gives the baseman only a minimum space to tag out. But the hook slide is a dangerous thing for an amateur, for it offers all sorts of opportunity for injury. A fraction of an inch error in judgment may mean missing the bag entirely and an easy putout for the opponents. More serious than that, however, is the danger of catching the bag with your spikes instead of the toe, in which case the ankle bones will be snapped off like twigs. Each season sees three or four men out of the game with broken legs or twisted ankles—and ninety-nine percent of such injuries can be traced to bad sliding.

If you start your slide too soon you are an easy

out. If you start too late there's always the danger of personal injury. Timing is just as important in sliding as in hitting, and lack of timing means a bad slide. To become a good slider there's only one method. That's constant practice. I can remember when the sliding pit was an important feature in every training camp—and rookies were sent out to practice for long stretches at a time, and under the eyes of experts. They don't do that much any more —not that practice is any less important, but because the slide and the steal no longer occupy as important a place as once they did in baseball.

To be a good slider a man must learn to hook the bag with either foot. That sounds easy, but it isn't. Just as a man is naturally right handed or left handed, so does he slide from the right side or the left side. And learning to "fall away" to either side equally well is a tough job that requires a lot of work.

A few years ago there was a lot of talk of "spiking." That has all gone out. No longer do men come driving into the bag with nasty spikes raised high ready to cut down the baseman or drive him out of the line of play. Old timers may make a bluff at "spiking " to try and frighten some rookie baseman, but I don't believe there has been a deliberate case of spiking in the big leagues in the last five years. Naturally men will get cut once in awhile accidently. One of the commonest plays on which "spiking" occurs, is on a high throw to the base where the baseman jumps in the air for the ball at the same instant the runner slides into the bag. As the baseman comes down he is apt to land on the runner with his spikes. But if the runner hooks the bag instead of going straight in, there is less danger in the play.

I was talking to one of the veteran newspaper men a few months ago and he told me an interesting story of how the spiking practice first originated. He gave credit (?) for the play to Patsy Tebeau, manager of the famous Cleveland Spiders of thirty years ago. Tebeau in his eagerness to win ball games conceived the idea of spiking.

"Go into their basemen tomorrow spikes first, and rip their legs off if you have to," Tebeau ordered one day, after four of his men had been nipped stealing.

The next afternoon one of Tebeau's runners followed orders, and ripped a four-inch gash in the second baseman's leg. Another leaped into the shortstop and tore a mass of skin off his shinbone.

"That will put fear in their hearts," Tebeau gloated.

SPIKING

He was right. Basemen, fearing the spikes, became mighty careful and the Spiders ran wild on
the bases through game after game. But accounts
were soon squared. In Pittsburgh following a game
in which Tebeau's players had gashed and cut three
of the Pittsburgh men.

In those days the players dressed at their hotels,
and it so happened that the Spiders had to go past the
Pirate hotel to reach the ball park. Just before the
Spiders were due to pass William Temple, owner of
the Pittsburgh team, assembled his players on the
porch.

"Here's a nice new file for each of you," he told
them. "The very minute that Spider outfit comes
along I want all you boys to be busy filing your spikes
—and keep filing them until you get a razor edge."

A few minutes later the Spiders arrived. Tebeau
ordered the bus stopped. He climbed out, walked
over to the spike-sharpening crew, and watched them
for a minute. Then without a word, he returned to
the bus.

"Never mind any spiking stuff," he announced to
his club later. "We'll get the worst of it. They've
got the sharper spikes."

The Pirates waited for the Spiders to open their

famous spiking attack. The Spiders didn't. So the Pirates decided to start the action. They began to hurl themselves into the bases regardless of results. The Spiders, knowing what the rival team was wearing on its feet stepped away from the bags and let the Pirates run bases free and easy. The Pirates scored fifteen runs that afternoon.

Naturally other clubs, seeing the success of the move, decided to do likewise. And so began the "spiking era" in baseball. The Baltimore Orioles were particularly good at it. And the extent to which "spiking" developed before finally it was barred by league rule can be illustrated by a story of Kid Gleason's, the peppery little second baseman of the old Orioles and later manager of the White Sox and now assistant to Connie Mack.

"Once" the Kid relates, "there was a third baseman who violated one of our spiking rules. He stuck 'em into the second baseman's chest. That was most unethical, inasmuch as one of our unwritten laws barred spiking ABOVE the waist line.

"The second baseman vowed to get revenge. Two innings later this particular second baseman having reached second, started for third on a drive through the infield. He probably could have scored on the play—but that wasn't his purpose. As he rounded third base he knocked the baseman down, faked a fall himself, recovered and slid back to third. In doing so he was very careful to slide his spikes right into the face of the third baseman."

"Those," the Kid always adds when he tells the story, "were the good old days."

May be so. But present day ball players have more good sense. They realize that such tactics, with the injuries that follow shorten careers. And the professional baseball career is short enough anyhow. Play hard, play fast, but play fair is today's motto. Intentional spiking has gone out, along with the emery ball and the ball park saloon.

CHAPTER XVII

Huggins a psychologist—How he put it over on the Pirates in the world series—Baseball superstitions—McGraw turns one to advantage and wins an important series—College men in baseball—What they have contributed to the game—Ball players who make good outside of baseball —Zane Grey once a professional—Billy Sunday and Governor Tener.

THE 1927 world series proved that baseball men don't come any smarter than Miller Huggins, manager of the Yankees. Hug pulled three things in that series that stood out like the warts on a pickle.

The first one happened the day before the series opened. We were to work out in the Pirate Park, and the Pirates had their workout just before we took the field. We came out from the club house. Most of the Pirates had dressed and were sitting in the stands to watch us go through our practice.

Hug spotted them at once. He called Pennock and Shawkey over.

"Listen," he said. "Those fellows are out here

PERFECT SLIDING FORM AS SHOWN BY TY COBB, WHOM BABE CALLS THE KING OF BASE RUNNERS. NOTE HOW COBB LEAVES ONLY A TOE TO BE TAGGED AS HE GOES INTO THE BASE. GEHRINGER OF THE DETROIT TIGERS IS THE BASEMAN WHO FAILS TO TAG OUT HIS FORMER MANAGER.

HERE'S ROSS YOUNG, FAMOUS GIANT OUTFIELDER, SLIDING SAFELY TO SECOND IN THE 1924 WORLD SERIES. YOUNG WAS ONE OF THE FEW MEN TO USE THE HEAD FIRST SLIDE SUCCESSFULLY

to watch us so we'll show them something. You two fellows will pitch hitting practice. When you go in there lay that ball right down the middle. Don't put anything on it. Let's show those fellows some real hitting!"

Combs was the first man up. He plunked the first pitch into the center field stands. Koenig swung twice, bouncing one ball off the right field wall, and the other off the left field barrier.

Then I came up. Bob laid them right down the middle, with just enough speed to make them perfect. The first ball I hit over the roof of the right field grandstand. I put another one into the lower tier. Then I got hold of one and laid it in the center field bleachers.

I was about to quit but Huggins walked over past me.

"Hit a couple more Babe," he whispered. "We've got them talking to themselves."

I hit two more long ones and gave way to Gehrig. Lou broke the fence with three swings.

The Pirates were flabbergasted. A friend of mine—one of the newspaper men who was in the stands—heard them talking.

"Boy, did you ever see such hitting?" Pie Traynor said. They're even better than they're advertised!"

The upshot was that the Pirates left the park that afternoon half licked before the series ever opened. They came out there to see if we hit as hard as everybody claimed, and smart little Hug spiked them in the first ten minutes.

Hug's second smart move came after Hoyt had won the first game. Everyone expected him to start Shocker or Pennock. He crossed them up.

"We'll start Pipgras" he announced in the clubhouse. "The fact that we think so little of Pittsburgh as to start a green kid, will get their goats. We've got 'em guessing now about our hitting. Putting in a kid pitcher against them will just about settle things. George goes in that second game—and if he gets away with it, we've got 'em. The series will be over in four games!"

You know the history of that series. Pipgras not only started but he had the Pirates under his thumb from start to finish. He won easily. The next day Pennock took them over the jumps—and that was a crowning insult too. For most of the wise guys had said that Pennock wouldn't even start since the Pirates were death on left-handers.

HUGGINS A PSYCHOLOGIST

Hug's wisest move, however, came in the final game.

It was the ninth inning, the score was tied, and we were going to bat for the last time. Combs singled and Koenig was safe when Traynor failed to come in for his bunt in time. I got a base on balls. Bases full. Nobody down. It looked as though the old series was in the bag.

Lou Gehrig came up. Lou was overanxious to hit—and John Miljus as wise and cool as pitchers come, worked carefully. Gehrig fanned. Meusel was up.

The boys on the bench were nutty.

"Put on the squeeze play," they urged Hug. "We've got to get Combs home. Let's try the squeeze!"

Hug grinned.

"Nothing doing," he said. "Listen to me. That fellow out there (Miljus) is trying too hard. He's putting too much on that ball. If someone doesn't hit he'll wild pitch sure. We can't miss. A hit or a wild pitch!" Meusel fanned and then—well it's an old story now.

With Lazzeri up Miljus cut one loose that was out of Gooch's reach. The ball swept past him and rolled to the backstop. Earl Combs, perched and ready to go at third, came galloping home with the run that won the game and the world series.

Miller Huggins had called the turn!

"Got to hand it to you Hug," Pat Collins piped up, "That's calling 'em better than I ever saw. You're a wizard!" Huggins grinned.

"Wizard, nothing," he said, "That's just baseball. It was bound to happen and I've been around long enough that I've learned to look for that sort of thing."

It just goes to show how a real manager takes advantage of every little thing to aid his team. Fellows like McGraw and Huggins eat and sleep and drink baseball. It's their very life—and the years give them a knowledge that can't be beat.

I don't know whether people realize it or not, but most ball players are superstitious. McGraw once capitalized superstition to win a tough series from the Cubs. To understand the story you must understand that one of the general superstitions of baseball is that empty barrels mean basehits. A load of empty barrels is one of the best signs a baseball players ever sees, and even a cross eyed umpire or a black cat can't jinx him after that.

BASEBALL SUPERSTITIONS

At the time the Giants had been in a terrible hitting slump. They were worried about it. They switched caps, they mixed the bats, they carried rabbits' feet. Nothing seemed to help. But one afternoon two or three of the boys came in the clubhouse grinning.

"Just saw a load of empty barrels," they said, "today the old slump ends."

That afternoon these fellows, inspired with new confidence, started hitting again. The next afternoon two or three more of the boys saw the barrels and the next day still others. For a week truck loads of barrels kept going past the clubhouse, and the boys all started hitting.

Which should be the end of the story. But it isn't.

A few days after the incident a big burly fellow in overalls came to the clubhouse and asked for McGraw. He was told that McGraw was out.

"Well I want my money," he grumbled. "I've been driving past this place with a load of barrels every day for a week, and I haven't had a cent of pay yet. I want my money!"

The boys naturally were wised up. Old Mac had hired a teamster to drive past with those barrels just to give the boys confidence and bring them out of their slump. He had fought superstition with superstition and won. That's smart managing.

One of the most famous superstitions in baseball is Eddie Collins and his chewing gum. For years, ever since he broke into the league I guess, Eddie has carried a wad of chewing gum on the button of his cap. And when he's at bat, the minute the pitcher gets two strikes on him, you'll see him step out of the box, take the chewing gum from his cap and start chewing it. He's done it so long now that it has become a habit. It's the only time he ever chews gum. And when he has finished his turn at bat, whether it's a hit or a putout, back on his cap goes the chewing gum. And it stays there until some other occasion arises when he has two strikes on him.

Urban Shocker believes that throwing a hat on a bed is bad luck. He used to room with Tommy Thomas, the kid pitcher, and one night Tommy came into the room, and threw his hat on the bed. Shocker was scheduled to pitch next day. And he was furious. The things he said to Tommy wouldn't look good, even if printed in Yiddish. It's a wonder Tommy came out alive. And it's a certain cinch he has never thrown his hat on the bed since then. The following afternoon Shocker pitched a beautiful game but lost by one run.

Joe Dugan has a queer superstition too. Joe will never throw the ball back to the pitcher. If you watch him in infield practice you'll see him throw to the plate, or second or first, time after time. But never to the pitcher. Once or twice the boys have tried to make him do it. Every time Joe would shoot the ball to a baseman, they'd throw it right back at him. Finally, seeing what was up, he delivered the ball into the pitcher's hands. But did he throw it? He did not. He simply walked across the diamond and handed it to him, then walked back to his post.

However the boys aren't as superstitious now as they used to be. A lot of the old-timers say it's because there are so many more college men in baseball now than there were a few years ago. Personally I don't believe that. The college players we get are just as superstitious in their own way, as the rough-necks who never attended college.

But college men have had an influence on baseball. And a good one. They've raised the game and the players. They've been responsible for cutting out a lot of the old-time rough stuff. And they've made baseball a real business in which men get good salaries and save it. In the old days when a baseball player finished his career he usually was down and out.

The money he earned he spent as fast as it came. Once he was through he was dependent on his friends and acquaintances for a job and a living. The college fellows have changed all that. They came into the league with a pretty good idea of what it was all about. They saved their money. And the other fellows followed their example.

There have been some great college men in baseball. Fellows like Mathewson and Eddie Collins and Jack Combs were the pioneers. Today there isn't a team in either league that hasn't several college men on its roster, and clubs are watching the colleges more and more for likely looking players.

The Yankees have Combs, Thomas, Gehrig, Gazella, Hanson and Dugan—all college men. Cy Williams is a college man. So is Ted Lyons. Gordon Cochrane, Muddy Ruel, Eddie Farrell, Max Carey, Jigger Statz, Hank DeBerry, Ernie Wingard, Ownie Carroll, Joe Sewell, Luke Sewell, Eppa

COLLEGE MEN IN BASEBALL

Rixey, Art Nehf, Travis Jackson, Gink Hendrick, Doc Gautreau, Vic Aldridge, Riggs Stephenson, Cliff Heathcote, Ray Blades—all of these are college men. And they're only a few of the scores who have gone into big league baseball and have made good.

Some people argue that college men are better ball players than the others. I don't believe that. But I do believe that the boy who has gone through college is quicker to learn inside baseball. He's more willing to learn too. The sandlotter, a lot of times, is a stubborn cuss who doesn't like instruction. The average college fellow realizes that he doesn't know it all and is willing to take advice from the players who have been around longer than he has.

But regardless of that, the other thing still goes. College men have been a mighty good influence in big league baseball and always will be. They bring wider training into the game. Muddy Ruel, for instance, is a lawyer who practices his profession in the off season. Bluege of the Senators is a certified public account. Art Nehf is an engineer, Eddie Farrell is a dentist. And by their example they prove to other ballplayers that there's something in life after the baseball career is over.

Of the present crop of big leaguers, there will be very few who won't be fairly independent when they have finished their career. Of course we can't all be Ty Cobbs. Ty quit the game with a million dollars—and that's more money than most professional athletes will ever see. But let me make this prediction.

In the years to come you won't see many former ballplayers walking the streets. They'll have enough to live on—and comfortably. During their playing days they meet not only other ballplayers, but they come in contact with the business world as well. Many a poor country kid has found through baseball, a contact and a knowledge of the world that he never even knew existed.

Take the average country kid rookie who goes south in the Spring. He's green. He's unaccustomed to city life. He is embarrassed in the hotel dining room. But baseball is a great teacher. And after two or three seasons of play he's a polished product, capable of holding his own in most any company. And that isn't bunk. It actually happens.

A lot of fellows who started in as professional ballplayers have made good in other lines when their careers as ballplayers ended. Zane Grey, the novelist who writes so many western stories, was once a professional ballplayer. He wasn't a big leaguer—but he played the outfield for a Western League club for several seasons. He played on a club which Ed Barrow, now business manager of the Yankees, managed.

Billy Sunday, the great evangelist, also was a ballplayer. Billy played with the old White Sox back in the barroom days, and he's still quite a fan. I've talked to him several times and on several occasions he has been around to see us in training camp. And he likes baseball as much as ever. Lots of times I've seen him peel off his coat and vest, and get out there and hit fungoes to the boys for an hour at a time. And have a great time doing it.

Ex-Governor Tener of Pennsyivania, is an ex-pitcher. And a real fan. In baseball we have plenty of trouble with the umpires from time to time, but when all is said and done, they're a pretty fine outfit. Square shooters, all of them, honest and fearless and ready to fight for their decisions if necessary.

A lot of those umpires know more baseball than the players. Take a fellow like Tommy Connolly for instance. Tommy has been umpiring big league ball games for more than 35 years. He was in the National League for a long time, and he has been an American League umpire ever since the league was organized. Tommy was the last umpire to put me out of a ballgame. And that was way back in June 1922 when I threw dirt at him after he had called me out at second. I've learned my lesson now. I've found out that umpires are on the square, and that they want to give players all of the best of it if possible. It took a long time for me to learn—but rule number one in my book reads "Don't fight with umpires. It's bad business!"

CHAPTER XVIII

The men who play—What they are like off the field—Mere
human beings like other people—The road trips—Days in
the hotels—Fads and fancies—Koenig an expert pianist—
Hoyt a great reader—Huggins a financial student—Shawkey a great hunter—Baseball, with them, not a game but
a business—The men who play are business men.

WHAT are they like, these ball players? What do
they talk about and think about as they go traveling around the country? What do they do and say
off the playing field?

These are common questions—questions that are
constantly being asked by kids and grown-ups.

The answer is simple enough. They're much
the same as other men, interested in the same things,
living the same sort of lives. They are neither
better nor worse than the same number of lawyers,
or doctors, or business men, picked from the four
corners of the nation. They have their families,
their children and their homes to occupy their spare
hours.

They discuss politics, or finance, or farming or any other subject that appeals to the normal man. They eat, dress, sleep and live much the same as Mr. Smith the merchant, or Mr. Brown the banker. Which to many people will perhaps come as a surprise.

Come and visit the Yankees some evening, as they sit about the hotel after the game. Suppose it's in St. Louis, some hot night in mid-summer. You'll find Huggins and O'Leary and Fletcher sitting over in a corner, enjoying their cigars. Chances are they'll be discussing politics or the stock market. Huggins is a keen financial student. He reads all the financial papers and journals and follows the market as closely, almost, as a city broker.

And in Fletcher he has great company. Fletcher, during the off season is a successful middle Western farmer, the type of successful farmer who takes a hand in county politics: serves on the school board and is a director of the town bank. Fletcher does all these things, and holds all these offices.

Mark Koenig you'll find perhaps, playing the piano in the reception room. Mark does pretty well as a musician, and he plays not jazz but classical stuff. And if he's playing the chances are Waite

Hoyt and Benny Bengough will be around somewhere near, listening quietly, or perhaps doing a bit
of harmonizing. Benny is a musician too—in fact
he's engaged in giving me lessons on the saxophone
right now, and a tough job he has too.

Hoyt not only has a good singing voice, but he's
something of an actor as well. A lot of theatrical
folks who know, tell me that Waite could make a
success on the stage as well as in baseball. But he
isn't interested. During the off-season, instead, he
spends his time at his profession. He's a mortician,
and has an office with his father-in-law in Brooklyn.

Waite is a great reader too. I've been traveling
with him a good many years and I never saw him
start out on a trip without one and probably three
or four books in his bag.

Bob Shawkey is almost sure to be off in a corner
somewhere discussing his annual hunting trip. Bob
is one of the best hunters in the business, and knows
the moose trails of Canada as well as most of the
professional guides.

We have a lot of real movie fans on the Yankees
too. Lou Gehrig is a nut on movies, and usually
sneaks off to the nearest theater each evening. Earl
Combs likes them too, and Benny Paschal. Those

three are pretty apt to be together—though now and then Lou will pass up the movies to sit in on a bridge game with some of the rest of us.

We started a bridge game during the spring training trip of 1927 that lasted clear through the season. Gehrig and I played against Mike Gazella and Don Miller. Miller is the young pitcher from the University of Michigan who joined us last year.

You know most ball players are good card players. But on the Yankees at least, there is very little poker playing. Once and a while the boys will start a game. But pinochle and bridge are the two favorites. Gazella is a good bridge player. Ernie Johnson and Everett Scott were the champions when they were with the club. Pat Collins and Woodie, the trainer, are pinochle nuts. And they're always looking for a game.

Cy Moore and George Pipgras like to play "Hearts." It's a funny thing about Cy. He'll go out there on the mound before 50,000 raving fans, with the bases full and nobody down, and he'll be as calm and cool as though he was pitching hay. But put him down in a heart game and he's like a little kid. He yells, and shrieks and laughs until you can't stay in the same room with him.

BABE RUTH AND MILLER HUGGINS, MANAGER OF THE YANKEES, SHAKE
HANDS FOR THE CAMERA MAN AT THE 1926 WORLD SERIES

BABE RUTH TAKES A FEW MINUTES OFF TO COACH A YOUNG HOPEFUL
IN THE GENTLE ART OF HITTING

QUIET MEN AND "BARBERS"

Once on a western trip last season he got so bad that we ganged on him and put him back in the car with the newspaper boys. He had to promise to keep quiet before we let him come back to his berth.

The two quietest men on the Yankee club are Bob Meusel and Tony Lazzeri. They never say a word to anyone. At that I think Tony talks more than Bob does. I've seen Bob go through a whole day when I don't believe he spoke a word, unless it was at the dining table when he asked somebody to "pass the bread."

Fellows who talk a lot we call "barbers." Freddy Hoffman, the old Yankee catcher, was one of the best barbers I ever knew. Freddy would talk the arm off any one who cared to listen, and he didn't care what particular subject he talked about either. Earl Combs is another pretty good barber. Wallie Pipp, when he was with the club, was a champion. And what Wallie enjoyed more than anything else was to get hold of some baseball nut and then kid him into serious conversation about inside baseball. He and Joe Dugan would pull the stunt together. They'd get the poor guy surrounded, and get him to telling all his pet baseball theories.

"Gee," Wallie would say, "That's a great idea.

I don't know why no one ever thought of that before."

"Certainly is," Joe would chime in. "Now what
do you think should be done to stop a hitter like
Hornsby?"

The fellow would open up on that subject, and
when he was through Joe would probably remark:

"Say, you've certainly got the dope. I think you
ought to go around to Huggins and tell him about
that. He'd probably be willing to pay big money
for ideas like that."

I've seen Joe and Wallie spend a whole evening
just stringing some poor bird along—and they'd
have him so fussed finally, that he wouldn't even
know his name.

A lot of people still cling to the idea that professional baseball players are rough necks, hardly
fit to associate with real folks. And of course there
are good fellows and bad, among the players. But
then the same thing might be said of lawyers or
doctors or business men. Believe me, playing side
by side with a man through season after season, living with him in hotels, traveling with him on the
road, eating and sleeping with him month after

month, gives a fellow a pretty good line on just what sort of fellow he is.

And I say to you that in my experience I've found ball players to be just as much gentlemen as any class of men I ever knew. Nine times out of ten they're a lot better than the people who criticize them.

A couple of generations ago they may have been different. In those days the corner saloon was the hangout for the baseball crowd, and players who had finished their playing careers turned into bartenders. But they don't do it any more. Ball players are getting smart. They learned long ago that it takes pretty careful living and pretty steady training to keep up with the parade. I don't mean that ball players are plaster saints. They're not. But keeping in physical condition is just as much a part of their business as knowledge of discounts is of the business of a banker. And ball players today are business men first, last and always.

I'll never forget the disappointment of a friend of mine one evening in Detroit. He expressed a desire to see the players off the field so I took him around. He got his first shock when we went to the Book-Cadillac hotel. That's the newest, most expensive hotel in Detroit and one of the best in the country.

"Why the ball players don't stop at this hotel, do they?" he asked, with some astonishment.

"They certainly do," I replied, "and I'll lay a little wager right now that you won't be able to pick the ball players out from the rest of the guests either."

And he couldn't do it.

He recognized Meusel, for he had met Bob before. And he knew Gehrig. Once you've seen Lou down on the playing field you can't mistake those shoulders and legs anywhere. But the rest of them he didn't know. He was a surprised young man.

He expected the ball players to stand out from the rest—to be different. Maybe he expected to see a lot of loud-talking rough looking touts in caps and checked suits. I don't know. But anyhow, when I pointed the boys out to him, he looked a bit embarrassed:

"Why they look just like anyone else," he said, "They're just like ordinary people."

It's funny how a whole ball club will take up a certain fad. One fellow brings it around, and then the whole gang takes it up. The Yankees for a year or two, were nutty over cross-word puzzles. Walk into the hotel lobby and you'd see fellows sitting all around working puzzles.

Ward and Pat Collins were responsible for that. Then Merkle took it up, and Mike Gazella. Shocker got the craze, and the first thing you knew the whole club was doing cross-word puzzles. I suppose it was a fine thing. They certainly added a lot of new words to their vocabulary as a result. And I think I picked up a couple of jaw-breakers myself.

Mah Jong came near wrecking the Athletic team a few seasons ago. One of the fellows got a Mah Jong set and took it on a road trip. Before long every man on the club was interested in the game. They had six or seven sets of Mah Jong that they carried right along with them in the uniform trunks, and the boys used to start their games in the morning and run right through to game time. Finally it got so bad that Connie Mack had to call a halt—and I think he still blames the loss of the pennant on that Mah Jong craze.

Most ball players like all other forms of outdoor sport. Fishing and hunting are ever popular subjects of discussion. Lou Gehrig, for instance, would rather fish than eat. Lou never misses a chance to go cod fishing, and most any day in winter you'll find him out on the banks after cod. This college kid is one of the queerest ballplayers I ever knew. It seems he never feels the cold weather. The coldest day in winter he'll come swinging down Broadway without an overcoat, his coat open and no vest. Never wears gloves and half the time goes bareheaded. Some of the boys claim he never had an overcoat on his shoulders until he joined the Yankees.

Lou is a great eel-fisherman too, and in the summer after the ball game he will take his mother in his car and go shooting down to Long Island to spear eels. His mother pickles them and now and then she will send a big jar of pickled eels around to the clubhouse. Last year when the boys struck a big hitting stride they got the idea that it was the pickled eels which were responsible for their hitting and for more than three weeks they wouldn't go into a ball game until they all had taken a couple of bites of pickled eel.

The big leagues are full of players who are great hunters. Old Chief Bender, the Athletics' pitcher, was one of the best trap shots in the country, and the Chief can still handle a mean shot gun, long after his pitching days are over. Ty Cobb is a great hunter too—and at the end of every season he goes chasing off to the mountain country in Canada or the Western United States for a month of shooting. His home at Augusta, Georgia is filled with trophies. Among other things he has some of the finest bear and deer heads I've ever seen.

Other great hunters are Eddie Collins, Joe Bush, Sam Jones, Benny Bengough, Bob Meusel, Freddy Hoffman and Bob Shawkey. Shawkey is one of the best in the country and for years has been making annual trips into Northern Canada for a months outing after the season ends.

Eddie Collins is a queer hunter. Eddie likes to get out in the woods and tramp around with a gun, but so far as anyone knows he never takes a shot at anything. Eddie is too tender-hearted. He attempted to shoot a wounded deer once, but when the deer turned its head and looked at him sort of sad, Eddie hadn't the heart to pull the trigger. And I don't think he ever will. Anyway he makes the trip with the other fellows every fall, and during the season is one of the best conversational hunters in the business.

I like to hunt myself, but I'd sooner have bird

shooting to anything else. One of the greatest kicks I ever got in my life came last fall when I was out on Long Island with Bill McGeehan and Bozeman Bulger, the sport writers. For two days we lay around in the blinds without a single shot. Then a flock of geese came over and we got five of them. It's the first time I ever shot a wild goose, and I got as much thrill from it as I ever got from hitting a homer with the bases full. The best part of hunting, though, so far as a ball player is concerned, is that it keeps a man in fine condition. You can't tramp around over the country all day long, packing a heavy gun, unless you're in shape.

Golf is another game in which ball players are fairly expert. They say that Walter Hagen, the great golf pro, would have made a great ball player if he hadn't gone in for golf. Well, Jigger Statz of the Brooklyn Dodgers, can hold Walter even. Jigger has had plenty of opportunity to turn golf pro if he hadn't been in baseball.

Statz is about the best of the ball player golfers I guess. But there are some others who are almost as good. Poor old Ross Young, who died in San Antonio last winter, was one of the best. Bob Shawkey is a fine golfer, and so is Sam Rice of the

Senators. Nick Altrock is another boy who can play pretty close to par, and Dazzy Vance, Aaron Ward, Bucky Harris and Eppa Rixey are others who swing a deadly mashie.

One thing most ball players can do on the golf course is drive. They may be bad on their approaches, and their putts may be terrible—but they all of them can sock that old ball from the tee. One of the longest drivers I ever saw is Sam Jones, the pitcher. Sam doesn't know much about the game, and he isn't always sure which direction the ball is going—but he certainly can sock 'em from the tee.

A lot of big league managers forbid golf playing during the regular season. The story is that the golf swing ruins a player's hitting swing. Swinging at a stationary object like a golf ball, they say, ruins the timing in swinging at a moving object like a baseball.

Personally I never noticed it, and I play a lot of golf during the year.

And if you ask me, the chief objection managers have to golf isn't the actual playing at all. It's the conversation. Golf is one of the "talkingest" games in the world. If fellows would go out in the morning and shoot their eighteen holes, then come in and keep quiet it would be alright. But they don't do it. They play the game over again each afternoon on the bench, and it gets a manager's goat to have some guy doing an imaginary mashie shot from a trap right when there's important business out on the ballfield.

What I've tried to show in this chapter is that the big league ball player is much the same as any other human being. He lives his own life; has his family, his home, his hobby and his outside interests just the same as the banker, the clerk or the professional man.

Baseball is his life work and he studies it carefully. Thrown in a mixed crowd your baseball man will talk politics, or finance or any other subject that average men discuss. But put three or four ball players together and they talk—baseball. Laymen I know find something fascinating in the thought of a big league ball club traveling around the country. To the outsider, those hours on the train together, and the hours in the hotels are a sort of magic.

To us they are only routine. We have a lot of fun because we're all good fellows together. Card playing is a favorite pasttime while traveling. Music helps to pass away many hours. For the past

THE ROAD TRIPS

six or seven seasons I have never made a single trip
that I didn't take with me a portable phonograph
with a couple of dozen records. And from the time
we get on the train until we leave, that phonograph
is working overtime.

The boys frequently organize quartets and many
a bit of close harmony has been carved out in a
Pullman smoker.

What do we do while traveling?

Here's a typical scene. The club is enroute on
a long jump, say from St. Louis to New York.

In one section a card game is in session. Meusel
and Bengough, Ruether, Koenig, and Lazzeri are
playing "black jack." They have their coats off,
their collars discarded and their shirts open at the
neck. They're kidding and laughing over the
game. The colored porter stands by watching the
fun, and the conductor stops on his rounds to "sit
in" for a few hands.

Down the car a bit Hoyt sits reading a book.
Further on the fussy foursome is busy at bridge.
That's Gehrig, Miller, Gazella and myself.

Shocker is reading the newspapers, and his berth
is messed up with a dozen sports pages, torn from
as many different papers. Now and then he makes

267

some discovery and pauses to discuss baseball with Pennock who is writing letters across the isle.

A hearts game is going on at the far end of the car, and above the noise of conversation you can hear Cy Moore shouting and laughing like a little kid as he passes Combs the queen. Pipgras is in the game and Paschal and a couple of the newspaper men.

In an adjoining section Jules Wera is giving the phonograph a workout, and occasionally Koenig pauses in the business of playing cards to lift his voice in the chorus of some song the phonograph is playing.

Pat Collins is busy over a cross-word puzzle, and cusses Woodie out when the trainer pesters him about starting a pinochle game. There's the tapping of typewriters as a couple of the newspaper men pound out their yarns for early editions.

Through the open door of the drawing room you can see Huggins, smoking his pipe and talking with O'Leary and Fletcher his assistants. Thomas comes along and slaps Wera with a folded paper and Wera in return smears him with a pillow. They tussle about the car.

Out in the smoking room some of the boys are

THE ROAD TRIPS

whooping it up on "Sundown" with one of the newspaper men playing a harmonica accompaniment.

Fun? Sure, it's fun. And the reason is that we're all one big gang together. We know each other, trust each other, like each other. Baseball has had its share of wonderful friendships and most of them have started aboard rattling, old Pullman cars when the boys get a few hours to themselves and have a chance to act natural.

CHAPTER XIX

THE average fan, eating peanuts in the grandstand
and cheering or jeering the players as the mood
strikes him, looks upon professional baseball as a
sort of daily circus for the men who play.

"Gee, what a soft job you fellows have" they say.
"Getting paid for going out there and having fun
every afternoon—and big money, too!"

I never hear a remark like that but I think of that
day, back in 1914, when I signed my first contract
and Brother Gilbert gave me his first words of
fatherly advice:

"Playing baseball on the sand lots is one thing
George" he said. "And playing professional baseball is something else. The sand lot game is just

boyish fun. You can start and stop as you please. Professional baseball is a business. It's a job for men."

Never were truer words spoken than those.

Certainly we (I mean professional ball players) have fun at our job. No man can make a success as a ball player unless he enjoys his work. But it is work—just the same as banking or practicing law or medicine is work. And we enjoy it in the same way other men enjoy their professions.

And we do get paid, and good money.

But, and here's the rub. Ours is a short lived business. At the age when most men are just reaching their prime we're through and out. Grown old at thirty-five sounds strange to most men, but the statement is all too true to the ball player.

Men sometimes envy us for the publicity we get and the fame. It is pleasant to see one's name played up in the papers day after day: there is a satisfaction in being recognized in the crowd and cheered perhaps. It's human nature to enjoy a little boosting —and ball players are only human. But there's another side to publicity too, a side which denies you all privacy, and makes your slightest mistake the subject for common gossip. General opinion is that ball players are rough necks, that they play the game fast and loose. That's wrong. They're not any better and certainly no worse than the average man in the street. But there's this difference. Everything they do or say or think is held up to public view.

Believe me publicity is not always pleasing or desirable. I know. A few years ago I sat in a Boston Hotel and saw "Red" Grange, broken, and nervous. Deep lines were under his eyes, his fingers trembled and his nerves were on point of breaking. All because he was being hounded by men whose friendly publicity was actually wrecking him physically. Right off hand I can't think of any two young men who have tougher jobs to fill than Colonel Charles Lindbergh and the Prince of Wales. Never a chance to be alone, never a chance to make a move that isn't the subject of public discussion the moment it is made.

Don't misunderstand me. We all like favorable publicity. And no matter how much we get, we still enjoy it. I've had a lot of it. Most of it good, some of it bad. And I confess that most of the bad was deserved.

I only bring up the point as answer to those men and women who, sitting comfortably in the grand-

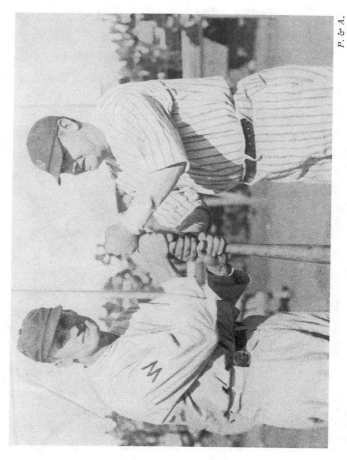

P. & A.

BABE AND WALTER JOHNSON, KING OF SPEED BALL PITCHERS, CHOOSE UP SIDES FOR A SAND-
LOT GAME DURING THE OFF SEASON

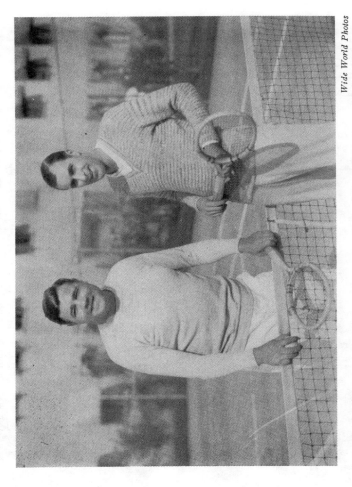

TENNIS IS A GREAT CONDITIONER. HERE ARE BABE AND "BIG BILL" TILDEN READY TO DO BATTLE ON THE COURTS IN HOLLYWOOD

stand and watching the ball game, envy us our jobs without realizing just what those jobs mean. Baseball, has its unpleasant side along with the pleasant: it brings its worries along with the laughs: its troubles along with its joys.

You sit up North shivering in the snow and cold of February and March, and read perhaps of the warm Florida sunshine, the fine hotel meals and the men in training for baseball. And you envy them, which is natural.

But there's another side to the picture—a side which isn't so attractive. That's the side of sore and aching muscles driven almost to the point of breaking; it's the side of sore arms and legs and aching feet that plow and fight the Florida sand in an effort to gain condition. There's the story of families left behind for six weeks or two months at a stretch, and then deserted again during the summer months when the professional ball player spends his days and his nights on the road.

The fan forgets these things for publicity has made the ball player something a little different from human. But the players themselves know, and I've heard them sit cussing the very fate that turned them into ball players and kept them living the life of roving gypsies for seven or eight months out of the year.

That is not yet a complete picture. For in the case of the young ball player there's also the ghost of failure just around the corner. Men talk of this or that profession as being a tough one in which to make good. Baseball, or more particularly big league baseball, is the toughest in the land. Out of 400 rookie players who go South each spring with their hopes high, not more than 10 make the grade. The rest—well, they just disappear. Maybe they come back three or four years later, older and wiser. Perhaps they never come back at all. They're just swallowed up into the unknown.

People sitting in the stands, think little of the unpleasant side of baseball as a profession; or if they think of it all dismiss it with a shrug of the shoulders and the statement: "Oh well, if he wasn't a ball player he'd probably be digging ditches, or working on a farm."

That attitude has always struck me as most unfair.

You know if Galli-Curci couldn't sing she might be doing hard tasks in her native land; if Booth Tarkington couldn't write books, he might be an

PROFESSIONAL BALL A REAL JOB

Indiana farmer or if Arthur Brisbane couldn't write editorials he might be a subway guard. Funny of course, but just as fair as the other.

Don't misunderstand me. I'm not knocking my profession. I went into professional baseball because I loved it, and the game has been more than good to me. But I am trying to outline the unpleasant side along with the pleasant. Then if any of the chance readers of this story have desire to play the game professionally—they will know the bad side as well as the good. Sand lot baseball is a lot of fun—simply because it's a game which you can take up or drop as you please. But professional baseball is a real job, the same as any other life work—a job that takes the best there is in you, and when you're finished, leaves you to carry on as best you can.

Once a ball player has made the grade, once he has broken down the competition and made a place for himself, his future is pretty much in his own hands. Smart men like Ty Cobb, Eddie Collins, Max Carey, Zach Wheat and players of that type have continued their careers long past the average length. The average big league career is eight years. These men have gone on for 15 or 20 seasons still playing the game. The answer, of course, is physical condition.

Keeping the proper physical edge is one of the most important things in baseball. Very frequently ball players are broken down physically before they waken to that fact. That's tragedy. I came near falling into that kind of tragedy myself. But I learned my lesson in the nick of time. In the past three years I have trained as conscientiously as a prize fighter. I have watched my diet carefully— and my weight. And I have played better baseball.

And it strikes me that the average man on the street, regardless of his profession, could take example from the laws of baseball training. Of course men can be divided into two general classes. On the one hand are the fellows of slight build—slim and wiry, who are always underweight rather than over-weight. Into this class fall most of the men who last longest in the big leagues. Their physical problem is one of building up rather than taking off weight. Carey, Cobb, Collins—all are of that type. Joe Dugan, Bob Meusel, Earl Combs fall in the same class. The other type are the fellows who naturally run to surplus flesh. I'm one of that sort. Lou Gehrig will be as he grows older. Harry

KEEPING A PHYSICAL EDGE

Heilmann, Bob Fothergill, Hack Wilson, and a dozen others in the big league have the same trouble.

And that's the deadliest thing in baseball.

A man's legs, you know, are the first thing to go in baseball. There's an old saying that "a ball player is just as old as his legs." Excess weight gives an added burden on the legs and wears them out just that much more quickly. Consequently the wise athlete watches that waist line—and so does the smart business man, if he is wise.

In avoiding excess weight the first thing to get right is the diet. The newspaper men kid a lot about fellows eating themselves out of the big leagues—but it's no joking matter. Lots of young fellows do it. We used to have a pitcher with the Yankees, I won't mention his name, who was one of the greatest eaters I ever saw. I've seen him eat three dollars' worth of food for breakfast, as much more for lunch, finish off the day with a six dollar dinner—and then complain of being hungry and go out for sandwiches and coffee before going to bed. That same fellow used to kick about his tendency to put on weight too. He's gone from us now—just a plain case of eating himself out of the league.

I used to have quite an appetite myself. I was

cursed with an iron constitution. And I really mean cursed. For my constitution was so strong that I could commit those excesses of eating without apparent harm for several years. When I did begin to have trouble, I had it in bunches and job lots. I eat a little fruit juice and toast and coffee for breakfast. I seldom eat lunch at all, and when I do I have only a vegetable salad of some sort. I eat one good meal a day and that's dinner. At that meal I have meat—but always with plenty of vegetables and green stuff. Two years ago if anyone would have told me that I could get along on so little food I would have said they were crazy. Now I do it day after day, and I not only feel well fed—but I'm stronger than ever. Which just goes to show that eating, beyond a certain point, is a matter of habit. It isn't necessary, and it isn't healthful.

Here's another tip. Take exercise regularly, but not too violently. I used to loaf around all winter putting on weight. Then I'd try to take off in two weeks of strenuous training, all the pounds that it had taken me the winter to accumulate. The result came mighty near being fatal. The minute a man, not used to exercise, goes into the thing too strenuously, he is putting a strain on the heart that's bound to make trouble. The heart weakens, that affects the digestion, the stomach goes bad and the first thing you know you're a fit subject for the hospital.

Exercise regularly but use good sense. And remember always that it's easy to keep in condition but it's a tough job getting back physical fitness that has once gone. Right now, well past thirty years old and supposedly on the down grade of my baseball career, I'm in the best physical condition I ever knew. The reason is that the minute the season ends I start in on exercises that will keep my muscles hard and my weight down.

My winters used to be full of vaudeville tours, movies and that sort of thing. But not any more. Right after the 1927 world series was over Lou Gehrig and I went on a barnstorming tour. We traveled all the way to the Coast, playing ball every day. After I returned I started on hunting trips. There's nothing like hunting to keep the legs in shape. The long hikes over the hills, the hours spent in the duck blinds, inhaling the bracing salt air— there's nothing like them. I've always found golf a great conditioner. And in addition to that I spend a couple of hours twice a week in the gymnasium. I play a little hand ball, box a little perhaps, and take exercises aimed at that oversized stomach. Nothing very violent—but regular.

And the answer. Well, I was broken in health three years ago. I lay for weeks on a hospital bed and most of the critics predicted that I would never play baseball again. But I did. And today I'm in the best physical condition I've ever known, and playing the best ball. Perhaps there will be some satisfaction in that for some of the tired business men who at thirty-five find themselves slipping physically. Certainly if I can do it, so can anyone else.

To the young man interested in baseball as a career, perhaps I can outline a few rules that are helpful. Learning to play the game is of the least importance. That's a natural thing. Either a man has ability as a ball player or he hasn't, and I take it for granted that no young fellow will plan a baseball career unless he is assured of his mechanical abilities.

But these rules are good always.

Study the game. Remember that baseball is a profession as intricate in its own way as the law or medicine.

Don't be afraid to accept advice. Other men can

always give you good pointers now and then no matter how much experience you've had. And there's always something new to learn. No one man ever knows it all.

Keep physically fit always. It isn't hard if you do it, but if you let yourself slip it's doubly hard to come back.

Most important of all—and this goes not alone for baseball but for every other profession—save your money!

Perhaps you say I'm a queer one to preach that gospel. Personally I'm fitted, I believe, above most everyone else. For I've played both sides. For several years I spent my money as I earned it. I threw it to the four winds, without thought of any future day or any idea of saving.

If I had saved from the start of my career I might have had a million dollars today. But I didn't. I'm not sorry, for what has gone before. It probably was good experience for a young fellow who never had seen the world or known anything about the world's people until he went into baseball.

But, boy, I'm glad I got wise to myself in time. From now on a part of my earnings each year go right down into the savings account. I don't know how much longer I may be able to play baseball. Perhaps for five or six years. Perhaps only two or three. You never can tell what another new season will bring.

Here's one thing that's certain.

I'll play just as long as I can. It's my profession, my life, and I love it.

And when I'm through I will be able to retire and live the way I want to live—knowing that I have plenty to support myself and family for the rest of my days.

And that's my baseball story.

Hereafter in thinking of baseball and baseball players I ask you to remember only that it's a great game, worthy of the best you can give it. And ball players, off the field, are much the same as you—just as human, just as friendly, just as much interested in their own lives, their own affairs and their own ambitions.

Some of us are a little rough, true enough, but then so are some of you. Some of us have lacked opportunities for education and training. So have some of you. But we're all good citizens, all of

AND THAT IS THAT!

average honesty and integrity; of average intelligence and average character.

We like the cheers when they come: we take the jeers as they echo. We try to give the best we can, and once we're too old to carry on we all hope to step down gracefully to bow to the youngsters who succeed us. Youth, you know, is the life of baseball —and we can't keep our youth forever.

And that, as the boys say, when they hit into a double play, is that!

CHAPTER XX

BASEBALL is full of laughs.

And full of good stories too—stories that go the
rounds of the camps, through the long seasons until
finally they become a part of the game itself.

A good many of our best baseball stories center
around the umpires, and the arguments over close
decisions. Fans, being quick to jeer, very frequently think an argument is going on, when there's
nothing of the sort really happening. Five times
out of ten when a player engages an umpire in conversation at the plate or on the bases, it isn't an
argument at all.

I remember an incident at the Stadium a couple of
seasons ago. Clarence Rowland was working back
of the plate, and early in the game he had called a
couple of "close ones" against the Yankees. As a

matter of fact his decision had been right both times —but that didn't make any difference to the fans. They were on him plenty.

Finally in the eighth inning I came up with two men on base. Earl Whitehill was pitching. Whitehill threw the first one.

"Strike one," Clarence yelled.

"Oh you robber," came the echo from the stands. Again he pitched. "Strike two," Clarence shouted.

"Robber. Bum. Thief!" These and other choice bits of comment came down from the stands and bleachers.

I stepped out of the batter's box and turned to speak to Clarence.

"That's right, Babe," the fans yelled, "tell him a thing or two. Give it to him." And the jeering doubled as we talked.

Finally the game ended and as I trotted across the field some big bruiser came bustling out of the stands and patted me on the shoulder.

"At 'a boy, Babe," he howled. "I guess you told that blind umpire a thing or two, eh? He's just a bum anyhow! Keep after him!"

Which was all right except for two things. In the first place Clarence had been right. Both balls were strikes. And in the second place I hadn't questioned his decision for an instant. What I had said was simply this:

"Did you see that one curve? I wonder where he got it. That guy never showed me a hook like that before!"

————

Half the laughs in baseball come from quick repartee, and the umpires are about as quick as anyone.

One of the funniest lines I ever heard, or one of the best come-backs, was pulled by Tommy Connolly, the veteran American League umpire. Bob Veach of the Tigers was the goat.

The Tigers were engaged in a tight game and Tommy had had more close ones than usual that day. It was hot too—and the boys were a bit crochety, and they were on Tommy plenty.

Finally Veach was at bat and got hold of one, sending it on a line over third base to the wall. Bob didn't stop to wait for the decision—just hit out down the baseline and he was on second base before the outfielder reached the ball.

Tommy called him back. "Foul ball," he said. "You'll have to do that one over."

ONE ON VEACH

Bob kicked plenty—but Tommy stood his ground.

At the end of the inning Veach went out to left field, took a look at the foul-line and came racing back to the plate.

"Say, Tommy, that ball was fair," he howled. "It landed right on the foul line. There's a mark in the lime where it landed. I can show it to you!"

Tommy dusted off the plate, then straightened with a grin.

"Well, well," he said, "is that so? Now I tell you what to do. You run right out there and bring that foul line in to me. I'll take a look at it!"

Bob was stopped plenty. After that he never again tried to rag Tommy.

———

The players themselves pull many a good line too. Some of them are particularly expert—and there are few men in the league who have anything on Joe Dugan.

I'll never forget one he pulled in the 1923 world series between the Giants and Yankees. It so happened that in one of the games, Joe came to bat with two men on and a run needed to tie.

Big Jack Scott was pitching for the Giants.

At such a crucial moment as that ball players are

supposed to be nervous and excited. Maybe some of them are. But not Joe.

With the crowd howling and yelling he selected his bat and walked slowly to the plate. He dusted his hands deliberately and then stepped into the batter's box.

Scotty was all ready to pitch, but just as he started his windup, Dugan stepped out of the batter's box, held up his hand for time. The umpire motioned Scott not to pitch.

Then Dugan made a megaphone of his hands, and turning toward Scotty shouted out a line that I'll never forget:

"Hey, Scotty," he said, "pull in your ears. You look like a loving cup!"

And Joe got his base hit too!

———

As I said before the umpires figure in a lot of baseball's funny stories, true and untrue.

One of the best laughs I ever heard was the story told by my friend Bozeman Bulger, the baseball writer, concerning the colored umpire down in Alabama.

It seems that two darky teams were such bitter rivals that when they met for the championship it

Christy Walsh Syndicate

BILL DINEEN, THE UMPIRE, TALKS THINGS OVER. DINEEN WAS
ONE OF THE GREATEST OF EARLY DAY PITCHERS. HE STARRED IN THE
FIRST WORLD SERIES IN 1903, AND HAS A NO-HIT, NO-RUN, NO-MAN-
REACH-FIRST GAME TO HIS CREDIT

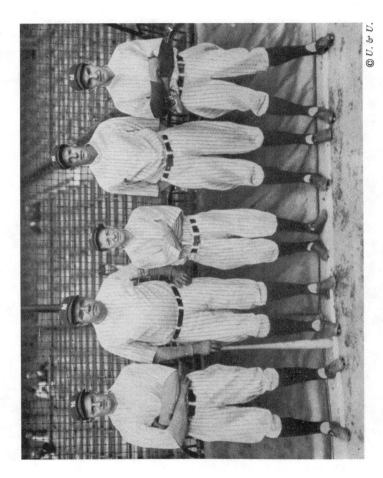

VETERANS OF THE YANKEE CHAMPIONSHIP ARRAY. READING FROM LEFT TO RIGHT: WAITE HOYT, RIGHT HAND PITCHER, BABE RUTH, MANAGER MILLER HUGGINS, BOB MEUSEL AND BOB SHAWKEY, KING OF CURVE BALL PITCHERS

was decided to send to Baltimore and get the fanciest umpire known to their circles—a cocky colored official of considerable reputation.

One of the teams had a gigantic first baseman who was also a terrific hitter. On the day of the battle this giant—Bam Sparks, they called him—eyed the little dried-up umpire from head to foot. Bam was not at all impressed by the Baltimore reputation.

The little umpire must also have had some doubts in his own mind.

Finally Bam Sparks came to bat. The first ball pitched split the plate and he didn't swing at it.

"Strike one!" screamed the little umpire with a wave of the hand that impressed the colored rooters if not the hitter.

Bam turned and quietly looked the imported umpire over, but said nothing. His grunt, though, was full of meaning.

A few moments later another strike came over.

"Two," screamed the umpire with the same trick swing of the arm, and his voice raised to a wail.

Bam Sparks quietly dropped his bat to the ground, spat tobacco juice in the dust and slowly turned around, giving the little ump a dirty dirty look.

"Two whut?" he demanded.

That one look did the trick.

"Too High," came the ready response, and Bam resumed his position at the bat.

———

Perhaps it was the same colored umpire who figured in that other game now so well known to the story tellers.

At least this one was a little fellow, colored and weazened, and he was umpiring the championship game between two colored contending teams.

It was a troublesome day. All through the game he had been in hot water, and as the ninth inning came around he was being threatened with everything from hanging to boiling in oil.

Nor could he expect help from the fans, for they were about evenly divided. The game was played on neutral ground and there was no home club to favor. He was on his own.

Came the last of the ninth inning as the movie people put it. The team in the field had a one run lead, the bases were full, two were out, and the count was three and two on the hitter.

The pitcher wound up and let the ball fly.

The batter didn't swing.

Instead he turned in his tracks and eyed the umpire. "That's a ball suah," he said with pretended certainty.

"Right through the plate," the catcher retorted, and there was murder in his eye as he turned to the umpire.

The ump was dumb for an instant, and his eyes were looking for the nearest exit.

The teams came clustering around.

"Well," they demanded, "say something. What was it?"

Again the little ump eyed the exit. His knees shook. His hands trembled.

"D-d-d-doubtful!" he howled finally, and broke for the gate. According to the story he's still traveling.

———

There's nothing ball players like better than to sit around the hotel lobbies in the evening swapping yarns. And at times like that they're not hampered by truth either. Two of the greatest storytellers I ever heard are Charley O'Leary and Sam (Sad Sam) Jones. Why anyone should ever call Sam "Sad Sam," is more than I can figure. He's one of the most cheerful, happy, even dispositioned fellows I ever knew. But that's beside the story.

I had the pleasure of sitting in on a confab in Washington one night when Sam and Charley were exchanging yarns. They had been going along for some time when Charley weighed in with this one.

"Two colored teams," he said, "were playing for the city championship of Chicago—a tough, tough game that finally went into extra innings. The game was played late in the fall, and darkness came along toward the last. Finally in the twelfth inning it was so dark that you could hardly see the ball.

"One team scored a run in the first of the twelfth, giving them a two to one lead. In the last half of the twelfth the other team filled the bases, with two down. There were two strikes and three balls on the batter. It was a fine time for strategy.

The big colored pitcher beckoned to his catcher who strolled out to the pitcher's box.

"Listen," the pitcher told him. "You take that ball. Now you go back of that plate and when I wind up and make my pitching motion you smack that ball hard into your glove!

He wound up—and pretended to let fly.

Bam! went the ball into the catcher's glove.

SAM JONES' YARN

"Strike three, you're out!" the umpire shrieked.

And at the sound the batter whirled in his place and confronted the ump.

"Oh you thief," he howled. "You call that a strike. Why that ball was two feet outside!"

———

Most of the boys were willing to give Charley the leather medal on that one. But not Sam. He had a counter-yarn that he sprung, and this was it.

"We used to have a pitcher out in Ohio who was a wonder at that trick motion stuff in catching men off base," Sam said. "He was one of those fellows who could throw equally well with his right hand or his left. Well sir, this fellow got quite a reputation around his part of the state, and finally got a job pitching for a semi-pro club that was playing for the championship.

"It was a tough battle. Neither side scored the first eight innings. Finally in the first of the ninth this pitcher's club put over a run. In the last of the ninth the thing got tougher. The opponents filled the bases with nobody out and the gang was shouting for the pitcher's blood. It was a tough spot.

"But did it bother this farmer kid? It did not. Know what he did?

"He strolled over to the bench as though he was getting a drink of water, and quietly picked up another baseball. Then he went back to the mound.

"Well sir, that fellow took a little windup and with his right hand he threw to first base, catching the runner there asleep. With his left hand he tossed to third base and caught that runner flat-footed too. And I'll be durned if his motion wasn't so deceptive that the hitter swung too, and struck out. Completed a triple play, right there, that pitcher did—and won the ball game.

"We grow our pitchers that way down in Ohio," Sam added and walked away. Charley was whipped. He had nothing more to say. That was once when Sam Jones had him stopped cold.

———

Getting back to truth again the boys tell a story on Rube Lutzke, the Cleveland third baseman, that gets many a laugh. I won't vouch for its truth, except to say that the Cleveland boys all tell it as fact.

You know a ball player loves his base hits more than anything in the world. When the official scorer gives him an error he takes it as part of the game. But let the scorer fail to give him a hit when he

A LAUGH ON RUBE LUTZKE

thinks he has it coming and there's a howl that you can hear all over the park. But I'm getting away from my story.

Rube, the boys say, had been going great at the bat for some time and finally he went into a game and came out with four hits in four times up. Naturally he was pretty happy, and he went home that night whistling and singing and laughing at everybody.

Mrs. Lutzke met him at the door and Rube was still whistling.

"Well," he says, "four for four today. Guess that's smacking the old pill, eh?"

A few days later hard luck busted Rube right in the eye. Seemed as though he couldn't get the ball safe to save his life, and in a double header one afternoon he went to bat nine times without anything that even looked like a hit.

Not so good! Rube scowled and muttered under his breath as he took his shower and got dressed.

Mrs. Lutzke met him at the door when he got home.

"Well, Rube," she said, "how many hits today?"

Rube was speechless for a minute, but finally he found his tongue.

"Listen," he said, "you attend to the cooking for this family and I'll do the hitting."

———

Most of the laughs in baseball come from wise-cracks pulled on the bench. Players rag each other a lot. "Jockeying" we call it in baseball. And some of the boys are expert.

Joe Bush was one of the best jockeys I ever heard. Freddy Hoffman, the old Yankee catcher, was another good one. Art Fletcher is no slouch either. And there are fellows on each big league ball club who make jockeying a real art.

Whitey Witt used to pull a lot of funny lines— not wise cracks particularly but just observations that had a lot of humor along with their common sense. Whitey's best one was pulled one day when we were playing Washington, and at Walter Johnsons' expense.

It was a tough game, and Walter had walked me intentionally when I came up with two men on and two out.

Whitey was on him in a minute.

"That's right, Barney," Whitey howled, "better four balls for one base than one ball for four bases anytime."

A GREAT GAME

That's one line that has gone around the league and back again. You still hear it dozens of times a season—a sort of unconscious tribute to Whitey Witt who finished his baseball career some seasons ago.

———

Yes, there are laughs in baseball—lots of them.

That's another thing that helps to make it a great game.

GLOSSARY OF BASEBALL TERMS

Barber—A ready conversationalist. Name applied to person who talks a great deal.

Jockey—a rider. Player who "rides" opposing players from the bench.

Taking him for a ride—ridicule and kidding of an opposing player in effort to disconcert him.

Horse collar—a zero in the box score hit column.

Cousin—a pitcher who is easy to hit.

Hook—a curve ball of any variety.

"Dusting off"—Making the hitter drop to the ground by pitching at him.

"Wasting one"—pitching outside and wide of the plate in an effort to head off a steal or prevent a hit and run.

"Leaning"—taking an exceptional long lead, preparatory to a steal.

"Breeze"—an easy chance.

"Texas Leaguer"—a fly ball just out of reach of the

GLOSSARY

infielders, but too close in for an outfielder to handle.

"Doing a Sammy Vick"—overeating. Sammy Vick was noted for possessing one of the most voracious appetites in the big leagues.

"The Syracuse Car"—the Pullman in which the rookies and substitutes ride. Originated with the Giants who used to play an exhibition game in Syracuse each year. Usually the second string men would play the game and their car would be shunted off at Syracuse while the others went on to the next big league town to enjoy a day off.

"Boot"—an error.

"A blow"—a base hit.

"In the groove"—a ball through the center of the plate, easy to hit.

"A sinker"—a fly ball that has a back spin which causes it to sink to the ground quickly.

"Rookie"—a first year man or a player who has not won his spurs as a regular.

"Whittling"—term applied to pitchers who attempt to fool hitters with balls just off the corner of the plate. A whittler is a pitcher who mixes up balls with strikes and carries a batter along to a two-two or three-two count before making him hit.

"Bean ball"—a pitched ball thrown at a batters' head.

"Giving it the old college try"—playing to the grandstand or making strenuous effort to field a ball that obviously cannot be handled.

Scribes—the newspaper men who accompany a big league ball club on the road.

Four for four; three for two, etc—the ball player's way of saying four hits in four times up; two hits in three times up, etc. An abbreviation of "three times up for two hits."

"Fungo"—fly balls hit to the outfield during fielding practice.